Hezekiah Butterworth

Zigzag Journeys in the Orient

The Adriatic to the Baltic; a journey of the Zigzag club from Vienna to the Golden

Horn, the Euxine, Moscow, and St. Petersburg

Hezekiah Butterworth

Zigzag Journeys in the Orient
The Adriatic to the Baltic; a journey of the Zigzag club from Vienna to the Golden Horn, the Euxine, Moscow, and St. Petersburg

ISBN/EAN: 9783744797078

Printed in Europe, USA, Canada, Australia, Japan

Cover: Foto ©Andreas Hilbeck / pixelio.de

More available books at **www.hansebooks.com**

IN

THE ORIENT.

THE ADRIATIC TO THE BALTIC.

A JOURNEY OF THE ZIGZAG CLUB FROM VIENNA TO THE GOLDEN HORN, THE EUXINE, MOSCOW, AND ST. PETERSBURG.

BY

HEZEKIAH BUTTERWORTH,

AUTHOR OF "ZIGZAG JOURNEYS IN EUROPE," "ZIGZAG JOURNEYS IN CLASSIC LANDS," "YOUNG FOLKS' HISTORY OF AMERICA," ETC.

FULLY ILLUSTRATED.

BOSTON:
ESTES AND LAURIAT.
1882.

Copyright, 1881,
BY ESTES AND LAURIAT.

All Rights Reserved.

PREFACE.

THIS volume seeks to make clear the so-called Eastern Question to young people.

It is fully supplied with stories and illustrations, as it is the design that all of the Zigzag books shall be. That this method is acceptable to the young is proved by the sale of nearly fifty thousand volumes of "ZIGZAG JOURNEYS IN EUROPE," and "ZIGZAG JOURNEYS IN CLASSIC LANDS," and by the free use of these books in schools as collateral readings. While in this volume the writer seeks to amuse and entertain, his better motive has been to leave in the mind a correct understanding of the politics of Europe that depend on the Eastern Question, so that the reader may take a more intelligent interest in foreign political affairs.

The writer is indebted to GEORGE M. TOWLE, Esq., for a number of paragraphs that clearly explain the politics of the East, and to Miss EDNA DEAN PROCTOR, author of "A Russian Journey," for the last part of the chapter on St. Petersburg.

H. B.

CONTENTS.

CHAPTER
- I. A CURIOUS JOURNEY PROPOSED
- II. STORIES ABOUT CONSTANTINOPLE
- III. THE EASTERN QUESTION
- IV. MOHAMMEDAN WORSHIP
- V. VIENNA AND THE DANUBE
- VI. THE CRUSADES
- VII. THE STORY OF MONTENEGRO
- VIII. BULGARIA AND THE DARDANELLES
- IX. CONSTANTINOPLE
- X. THE BLACK SEA
- XI. SEBASTOPOL
- XII. THE COSSACKS
- XIII. MOSCOW
- XIV. NIJNI NOVGOROD
- XV. ST. PETERSBURG
- XVI. THE ASSASSINATION OF THE CZAR

ILLUSTRATIONS.

	PAGE
Tommy in the Barber Shop . *Frontispiece.*	
Alexander's Column	14
Nijni Novgorod	17
Women of Mitau	19
Women of Novgorod	20
Calmuck Tartars	21
Kirguis Tartars	23
A Tunguzian Dance at the Fair	25
Wallachian	27
Dervish	28
Interior of St. Isaac's Cathedral, St. Petersburg	29
Turkish Mosque	33
Fair in the Orient	37
A Mohammedan	40
General View of the Kremlin	41
Statue of Peter the Great	44
Russian Soldiers	45
Russian Veterans	48
Map of the Overland Route to the East	49
Map of the Suez Canal	52
Constantine	55
Huns on a Foray	56
Pilgrims to Mecca	57
Ancient Gate of an Eastern Town	59
Mohammedan Street Scene	60
Travellers and Palm-Trees	62
An Eastern Entertainment	63
Arabian Travellers	64
Mosque of Omar, Jerusalem	65
Interior Court of a Persian Mosque	68
Door of Mosque of Bou-Medina	69
Minaret of Semnoon	71
Gate at Erzeroum	72
Mosque at Hoogly	75
The two Bears brought into Court	77
The Bears recognizing the Goldsmith	78
Sultan Bajazet's Mosque at Broussa	79
An Eastern Scene	80
The Prater	82
St. Stephen's Cathedral, Vienna	83
The Belvedere, Vienna	85
Church of St. Charles Borromeo, Vienna	87
View of Lintz	89
Monastery of Mölk	90
View of Passau	91
Dancing Dogs	93
Little Violinist	94
The Danube at Lintz	95
The Quay and Castle at Presburg	96
" Moriamur pro rege nostro "	97
Bridge at Pesth	100
The Danube at Buda	101
Quay at Pesth	103
Citadel at Pesth	104
View in Vienna	106
"The Maid had changed her Mind"	107
The Doctor "*en déshabillé*"	108
The Doctor followed by the Bear	110
The Doctor chased by the Bear	111
" I have left myself all along the Way and have fallen all to Pieces "	112
Castle on the Danube	113
City of Belgrade	116
Fortress of Belgrade	117
Crusaders on their Way	118

ILLUSTRATIONS.

Title	Page
Allegorical Picture of Charlemagne	119
Crusaders perishing by the Way	120
Wayside Shrine in the East	121
The Victorious Crusade	122
Servian Peasants	123
Servian Head-Dresses	125
Priest of the Greek Church	126
George III.	128
"Thou art betrayed!"	129
Proclaiming the Crusades	134
Montenegrins	135
Among the Peaks	138
Montenegrin Cavalry	139
Montenegrin Boy	142
Senator of Montenegro	143
Black Mountains	145
A Montenegrin Soldier	147
Montenegrin Girl	149
Bulgarian Tramps	151
A Garden of Beauty	157
Hedjadj passing the Palace	161
Naam's Palace	163
The Sorceress	164
Naam's Garden	165
House of the Governor	166
House of Numan's Father	167
Constantinople	171
Golden Horn, from a Kiosque in the Seraglio	175
Parlor in the Seraglio	179
Dervishes	183
Horizontorium	184
Fountain in the Seraglio	187
National Emblem of Russia	191
Great Seal of Ancient Russia	193
The Winter Palace	197
View of Plevna	201
Trebizond Seashore	205
Erzeroum	209
Fortifications of Trebizond	211
Armenian Martyrs	213
Russian Marriage Ceremony	217
A Garden Scene	220
Charge of the Light Brigade	223
Voltaire	227
Diderot and Catherine II.	231
Capture of the Malakoff	235
The Young Soldier	238
Russian Worship	239
"A Dutch Skipper told it me many, many Year ago"	244
Mazeppa	245
Funeral of a poor Russian	249
Military Evolutions of the Russian Army	253
Krassnaya Square	258
Palace of Petrowsky	259
St. Nicholas Church and Gate	261
Czar Kolokol	262
Vassili-Blagennoy (Church of the Protection of Mary)	263
Granovitaya Palata	265
The Red Gate	267
Russian Sledges	272
A Cossack	273
A Droshky Boy	275
Nijni Novgorod during the Fair	277
Inhabitant of Nijni Novgorod	279
A Russian Gypsy	280
Card-playing in Barges on the Volga	281
The three Witches in the Cave	282
Bulgarian Beggar	283
Bears in a Siberian Village	284
A Baba Yaga	287
Convicts on their Way to Siberia	291
Village on the Route to St. Petersburg	293
The Cottage of Peter the Great	295
William III., Prince of Orange	296
A Monastery in Northern Russia	298
St. Isaac's Cathedral	302
The Exchange	303
Nevski Prospekt	305
Nicholas Bridge	307
Assassination of the Czar	309
Alexander II. lying in State	313
Inauguration of Alexander III.	317
Cronstadt	320

ZIGZAG JOURNEYS IN THE ORIENT.

ALEXANDER'S COLUMN.

ZIGZAG JOURNEYS IN THE ORIENT.

CHAPTER I.

A CURIOUS JOURNEY PROPOSED.

Tommy Toby Proposes a Curious Journey. — The Great Eastern Question. — The Wonderful Fair at Nijni Novgorod.

IN the first volume of the Zigzag Series of books, we gave an account of the travels of an American teacher and a class of boys in England, Scotland, Belgium, and France. The book was called "Zigzag Journeys in Europe," the teacher's name Master Lewis, and two of the boys were Tommy Toby and Wyllys Winn. In the second volume of the series, called "Zigzag Journeys in Classic Lands," the same class visited the scenes of their classical studies, — the provinces of the old Roman Empire, Greece, Sicily, and Rome, ascending Mt. Parnassus, and crossing the waters passed over by Ulysses, Æneas, and the Apostle Paul. This party of vacation excursionists were joined at Marseilles by another teacher of the school and three other boys. The teacher was Mr. Beal, and one of the boys, who had a very inquiring mind, we called Charlie Leland. We left these tourists at Rome.

It was midsummer. Nothing could exceed in beauty the deep, glowing splendors of the Italian sky. The evenings were delicious, and the boys wished to spend them in the public places.

"Where shall we go on leaving Rome?" asked Tommy Toby of Master Lewis, on the last evening the party spent at Rome.

"I shall take the Class to Florence to-morrow."

In former volumes, we have used the word CLASS to designate Master Lewis and his pupils, and we will do the same in this. The teacher was accustomed to speak of his pupils who made journeys with him as THE CLASS.

"But why need we so soon leave Rome?" asked Tommy. "It is nearly two months before the beginning of the school year."

"The air at Rome in the evening is malarious at this time of year, and the Class is so impatient of restraint, I do not longer dare to expose them to danger."

"But where shall we go from Florence?"

"We will consider that question when we arrive at that healthful city. Where would you like to go?"

"To Russia."

"To Russia? What has turned your curiosity in that direction?"

"I should then learn all about the great Eastern Question."

The boys, who overheard the conversation, clapped their hands at this unexpected answer. Of all the members of the Class, Tommy Toby was the least likely to desire to master political problems.

"'The great Eastern Question!'" repeated Master Lewis slowly. "Thank you for the suggestion. The whole Class ought to understand the question, and all of its bearings on European politics. When we are in Florence, I will explain this question clearly to you all. This is, in part, an educational journey, you know. But, Tommy, the boys seem rather to doubt the truth of your smart answer, and I myself think that such an uncommon thirst for knowledge on your part is almost too good to be true. What has interested you in the Eastern Question?"

NIJNI NOVGOROD.

"Perhaps he wishes to go to St. Petersburg to inquire after the Sick Man of Turkey?" said Mr. Beal.

WOMEN OF MITAU.

"Who is the Sick Man of Turkey?" asked Charlie Leland. "I have heard of him ever since I could read. Hasn't he recovered yet?"

"No," said Mr. Beal; "he is worse."
"Incurable?" asked Charlie.

WOMEN OF NOVGOROD.

"I think he is sure to die," said Mr. Beal.
"What ails him?" asked Charlie.

"The European climate don't agree with his constitution. He needs a change of air."

KIRGUIS TARTARS.

"Russia and Greece would help him to a change of air very speedily, were it not for England," said Master Lewis.

This conversation excited the curiosity of the boys, who gathered closely around Master Lewis, saying, —

"Please tell us about the Eastern Question."

"When we are settled in a cool hotel in Florence, I will do so," said Master Lewis. "But, Tommy, you have not yet answered my question, — 'What turned your curiosity towards Russia?'"

"I once heard father read to mother, when she was ill, a book called 'A Russian Journey.'"

"Well, was it interesting?"

"It was *gorgeous*. Father said it was 'a masterpiece of the picturesque Latin style.' I like a part of it."

"What part of it?" asked Master Lewis.

"The part of it that told about a great fair. This part begins with some poetry, and I have always remembered it."

"The poetry?"

"Yes."

"What is it?"

"It commences. —

"'Now, by the Tower of Babel,
Was ever such a crowd?
Here *Turks* and *Jews* and *gypsies*.
There —'

'There' — 'there' — There. I forget the rest. But I always remembered 'The Turks and Jews and gypsies;' and I used to think, if I ever travelled, *that* would be the place to which I would go."

The Class laughed.

"Now we have light indeed," said Mr. Beal. "He would like to go to the Fair of Nijni Novgorod."

"*That's* the place," said Tommy. "A very poetic name."

"The Fair begins about this time of year," said Mr. Beal, — "a little later."

A TUNGUZIAN DANCE AT THE FAIR.

"How long does it last?" asked Master Lewis.

"Nearly two months," said Mr. Beal. "Tommy's idea is not a bad one: if a traveller wished to see all of Europe and Asia represented in one place, why, the place of all others would be Nijni Novgorod in August. It is the most remarkable fair the world ever saw. Russians, French, English, Persians, Chinese, Cossacks, Tartars, noblemen, fine ladies, fabric-makers, peasant girls, all gather here, and—"

"And the Turks and gypsies," interpolated Tommy. "You forgot them. I think they must be very interesting."

"And engage in a traffic on the banks

WALLACHIAN.

of the Volga, that amounts to $25,000,000 annually," finished Mr. Beal.

"And they have puppet-shows every evening," added Tommy. "And the gypsies dance, and the dervishes *howl*, and the jugglers swallow their heads, and the Arabs tell stories; and what a boy cannot learn there is n't worth knowing."

DERVISH.

"I think *I* would like to go," said Charlie Leland.

"Charlie is becoming interested in the great Eastern Question," said Master Lewis dryly. "Perhaps he, too, would like to hear the dervishes *howl*, though I think that would not be very likely to happen at the Fair of Nijni Novgorod."

Here the conversation ended; but the boys had become curious to understand the Eastern Question, and to learn more about the great fair of the Russias.

INTERIOR OF ST. ISAAC'S CATHEDRAL, ST. PETERSBURG.

CHAPTER II.

STORIES ABOUT CONSTANTINOPLE.

Mr. Beal Tells some Remarkable Stories about Constantinople and the Strange Fair at Nijni.

LORENCE, beautiful Florence, the Fiesole of the poets, on the Arno! Here Savonarola preached and perished; here lived Galileo, Dante, Michael Angelo; here art piles itself on art, until its very loftiness is gloomy; the travelled foreigner hastens to it with gladness, and is slow to depart. Its air is balm, the sky is enchantment, and the society abounds in the winning graces of simple but elegant refinement.

We do not intend to describe Florence here. A part of our tourists made it the starting-point of a journey to Ober-Ammergau and Switzerland, as you shall presently be told, and should we prepare a volume of Zigzag Journeys in Switzerland, Germany, and on the Rhine, we should wish to give a chapter to Florence in that, in connection with the history of this part of the Class, and so omit the description of the city in this. Suffice it to say, the Class went to Florence, and in its salubrious air Master Lewis was relieved of all fear of Roman fever.

No sooner was the Class settled in Florence for a few days, than Tommy Toby renewed his suggestion of a journey to the East.

"I have been studying the map in my guide-book," he said to Master Lewis.

"Well, what have you found?"

"This," said Tommy, pointing to a pencil-mark route he had made on a piece of paper.

Master Lewis read slowly, —

"'Vienna — the Danube — Belgrade — Rustchuc — Constantinople — Sebastopol — Poltova — Kiev — Moscow, and — '"

"Nijni-Novgorod," said Tommy helpfully.

"Then St. Petersburg," continued Master Lewis.

"Then home," finished Tommy. "That makes a fine zigzag on the map."

"Very," said Master Lewis.

"And would be a really fine midsummer journey," said Mr. Beal. "You would go down the Danube amid some of the most beautiful scenery in Europe."

"It would be a rather expensive journey," said Master Lewis, "and there are but three boys whose parents gave me permission to act according to my judgment in the matter of routes and expenses. I had intended to return to England by the way of Switzerland and the Rhine. I would like to go down the Danube, make an excursion through the Turkish principalities, and then visit Russia, if it were practicable."

"I will return by the way of Switzerland with a part of the Class," said Mr. Beal, "and you can go East with the others."

"Of course I had thought before of these plans that Tommy has popped upon us, but I hardly deemed it prudent to mention it then. I will consider the subject."

"Did you think of Nijni before I spoke of it?" asked Tommy.

"Well, no, not exactly that; but the general plan — Constantinople — Sebastopol — Moscow — St. Petersburg."

"You have visited Constantinople, I believe," said Master Lewis to Mr. Beal.

"Yes, fifteen years ago, before the Sultan was shorn of his glory. The Sultan hardly dares to appear in the street now, and he worships

TURKISH MOSQUE.

in a private mosque. Then he went to the mosque in triumphal procession, and all the city bowed down before him.

"I well remember a scene I once saw there on a certain Friday, which day is the Turkish Sabbath. The Sultan, who is believed to be the representative of Mohammed on earth, was to go in state to the mosque. Crowds filled the streets. The road through which his august majesty was to pass was lined with soldiers. A great booming of cannon was heard on the Bosphorus, for the Sultan was crossing the Bosphorus from one of his summer palaces. From the time that he stepped into his royal caïque, until he reached the European shore, a continuous salute was fired from the Turkish men-of-war lying at anchor in the channel.

"Flags fluttered from all the shipping.

"He landed amid a flourish of trumpets, mounted a splendid black horse, and followed a procession of officers of state, who walked, leading their horses by the bridle, so as to make him the one prominent figure of the pageant. He was dressed in red fez, and wore a glittering uniform. He dismounted at the mosque on a piece of embroidered velvet, and entered the edifice amid the salaams of the officers. Such a going to church as that I never saw, nor such an exhibition of vanity. He seemed to think himself a god.

"I will tell you one or two odd adventures I had on my arrival at the city. If you should go East, they may be of service to you."

The Class gathered closely around Mr. Beal, while he related the story of

MY ANCIENT FRIEND "OSIP."

When I arrived at Constantinople, I expected to find myself a stranger in a strange city. I was no sooner free from the health officer than I was greatly surprised at the number of people who came on board the ship, gathered about me, and found in me a long-expected friend.

"I knew you were coming," said one of the most affectionate of these. "I have been looking for you several weeks."

"You? Who are you? I never heard of you before."

"I? Don't you know me? I am 'Osip.' Want a dragoman, sir?"

"'Osip?' I have no friends in Constantinople. I never heard that name before. 'Osip'?"

"'Osip' — old 'Osip.' I knew you as soon as I saw you. I am 'Osip.'"

Then my Sunday-school training came to my assistance, and I understood the meaning, — "I am Joseph," — and this was perhaps a long-lost brother, who had been watching for me at the harbor, and who had now come in his caïque to meet me.

I should, however, have dismissed Joseph at once, without stopping for further explanation, had not such a crowd of liars and vagabonds surrounded me that I hardly dared to move.

"English consul sent me, sir."

"American consul sent me, sir."

"I met you before, sir, — England."

"Backshish! Backshish!"

"Joseph," said I, "take me to the custom-house."

My other long-forgotten acquaintances at once deserted me, and I was taken by old "Osip" to the place of inspection.

"Are you sure you ever met me before?" asked I, on parting.

"Are you not *Captain Victor*, of the Royal Hussars?"

How grand that sounded! One would be almost tempted to let the matter pass after such a flattering question.

"No; I am an American," said I.

"An *American!* I beg pardon! What a mistake! I thought you were Captain Victor; you look like him. A noble man is Captain Victor, and a true gentleman. Always employs me. Liberal-souled man. Beg pardon, sir. Hope you will forgive me, sir. Pay, sir."

I say it with shame, but there was something so friendly in the flattery of this old liar that I paid him uncommonly well. I understood the trick perfectly, yet his friendliness so met the wants of my lonely situation that I was generously inclined towards him, though, when I came to consider the matter, my conduct did look to me like rewarding deception. I parted with my long-lost brother at the American consulate, and never saw him again; but I never hear the words, "I am Joseph," repeated, that I do not recall this unexpected meeting with "Osip."

"Have any of your friends ever visited the Fair at Nijni?" asked Master Lewis of Mr. Beal, after the boys had retired for the night.

FAIR IN THE ORIENT.

"Yes,— Senator D——. I think it was just before he was a candidate for President of the United States, but am not certain as to the exact time. He had a fearful experience, and I thought I would not tell it before the boys; all such dangers seem to be past now. He related a part of it to me once, as we were walking through Pennsylvania Avenue in Washington, towards the Capitol, and he stopped under the Senate wing for some minutes to finish it. I shall never forget that narrative.

THE AMERICAN SENATOR'S FLIGHT FROM NIJNI NOVGOROD.

Many years ago, the senator of whom I was speaking resolved to increase his knowledge of foreign affairs, political and commercial, by visiting Russia in midsummer.

Immediately on his arrival in Russia, his ears were filled with the news of the wonderful Fair at Nijni Novgorod, and he resolved to attend. He received every polite attention from the officers of the Russian government, and a carriage and courier were provided him to make the journey to the Fair. As he approached the fantastic summer town on the Volga, he was surprised to meet people of all neighboring nations, hurrying in different directions, — English, French, Jews, Tartars, Cossacks, gypsies, clad in every conceivable costume, speaking unknown dialects, but all wearing a common look of terror and anxiety.

He entered the town. Such a sight he never beheld. In the thousands of shops, the tea marts, the bazaars of silks and jewels, the yards of iron, amid the caravans of Asia and in booths of the Jews and camps of the gypsies, all was terror. He knew not what it meant. As greatly as the people and costumes differed, there was no difference in the aspect of anxiety on every face. The tradespeople stood guard by their goods, but the visitors seemed everywhere leaving the city.

Sick people were everywhere to be seen. They lay by the wayside, their fever fanned by the cool breezes of the Volga.

The courier drove past the church.

The senator saw that the ground around the church was full of people, — motionless people, shunned people. There were other people staggering towards the church.

The senator called to the courier, —

"What does this mean?"

"Don't you know? — the plague!"

"And those people?"

"They are dying of the plague. They have crept up to the shadow of the holy church to die."

"This is dreadful!"

"Your honor?"

"What?"

"What would become of you, if I should die?"

"Courier?"

"What, your honor?"

"Drive to Moscow. Fly!"

The road leading to Moscow was bestrewn with the sick and dying. Everywhere crowds were flying in terror. There were carriages of nobles and people of wealth, that were furnished with pictures of crosses and the Virgin, on which the eyes of the affrighted occupants might rest should death overtake them.

The senator at last saw with relief the towers of the Kremlin rising in the blue distance. He reached Moscow in safety, beyond the reach of the pestilential air. He declared that he could never forget the scenes of woe, horror, and despair that he witnessed during that ride.

GENERAL VIEW OF THE KREMLIN

CHAPTER III.

THE EASTERN QUESTION.

MASTER LEWIS EXPLAINS THE EASTERN QUESTION, AND MR. BEAL RELATES SOME MOSLEM STORIES.

NE delicious evening at Florence, Wyllys Winn said, —

"I have been reading what our books of travel say about the Eastern Question, and I confess I do not understand it at all."

"Perhaps Tommy can explain it," said Master Lewis.

"I do not wish to understand it *now*. I am going to find out all about it when *we* reach the East."

"If Wyllys would like the secret history of the Eastern Question, I can give it in a very few words," said Mr. Beal. "Peter the Great, who founded the Russian empire, left it as a mission to his successors to conquer Constantinople, and to make that city the capital of the Greek church. This the Russian Government desires to do."

"But why does it not do it?" asked Wyllys.

"Because Europe will not permit it."

"The subject now appears to me more dark and mysterious than ever," said Wyllys. "I do not understand — "

"What?" asked Mr. Beal.

"*First*, why Russia should be ambitious, with all of her great territory, to possess Constantinople.

"*Second*, why England and other Christian countries should side with the Turks against Russia."

"Your points are well made," said Master Lewis. "Let me try to make the subject more clear.

STATUE OF PETER THE GREAT.

"In the first place, let us recall three facts. One is, that Constantinople, the present capital of Turkey, was the seat of the Greek Church, of which the Czar of Russia is now the head, before the Turks invaded Europe.

"The second is, that a large portion of the inhabitants of Turkey are not only Christians, but are Sclaves; that is, of the same race and blood as the great body of the Russians themselves.

RUSSIAN SOLDIERS.

"The third fact to be kept in mind is, that for two centuries Russia has coveted Constantinople, not only because of her ambition that that city should once more be the capital of the Greek Church, but because she desires to be a great naval power. Now, the possession of Constantinople would give her the command not only of the Black Sea, but also of the Eastern Mediterranean.

"The Crimean War was the result of an attempt to make this conquest on the part of the Czar Nicholas; but England and France came to the Sultan's rescue, and Russian ambition was checked by the fall of Sebastopol.

"Russia still covets Constantinople, and is believed to be at this moment taking advantage of Turkey's difficulties with that end in view. She encouraged the rebellions in Bosnia and Bulgaria, and undoubtedly urged Servia to declare war against Turkey."

"But what concern has England, so far distant, in this trouble between Russia and Turkey?" asked Wyllys. "What cares she whether Russia takes Constantinople, or what becomes of the Sultan's rule?"

"She has two reasons for being deeply interested in the quarrel. In the first place, England is the foremost naval power in the world. She boasts that her navy is the greatest, and that her fleets rule every sea. She dreads to see Russia in possession of the Bosphorus, with a great port at Constantinople, rising to be a rival naval power.

"But she has a yet more powerful reason than this. England rules over the great empire of India. She is most anxious to maintain that rule, and will fight to the last to maintain it.

"Now, Russia has been for years approaching India with her troops by way of Central Asia, and her armies are almost in sight of the Indian frontier. There is little doubt that Russia is ambitious to possess India as well as Constantinople.

"Well, it happens that the nearest routes for England to India are through the Mediterranean, and by the Suez Canal. Suppose, then, that the Russians had Constantinople. Her fleets could sail freely on the Mediterranean, and might prove an immense obstacle in the way of English ships going to India. She might be able to cut off English communication with India by the nearest routes altogether.

RUSSIAN VETERANS.

"In case of a war, then, we should see the Russian fleet in the Mediterranean stopping the way of the English, while with her armies in Central Asia she made an attack on India.

"It is mainly this fear of losing India, and of Russia's getting it, that impels England to sustain the Sultan, and to resist a Russian conquest of Constantinople. Thus she fought for Turkey in the Crimean War, and will probably fight for her again, should her interests demand it.

"Open your guide books. Look on the map of the East. Let us have a geography lesson, and, before we finish the study, I hope you will more clearly see the meaning and the bearings on European affairs of the so-called Eastern Question.

"In the first place, let us consider more fully the question as to why Russia desires to conquer Turkey. It does not arise from the love of power alone, but, as you will see, from the traditions of a common ancestry and a common church.

THE CHRISTIANS IN TURKEY.

The Sultan's dominions in Turkey contain a population of about sixteen millions of souls. Of these, the Mohammedan Turks, who are the ruling race, to which the Sultan belongs, and of which he is the head, comprise only about three millions, while of Christians there are about twelve and a half millions. There are, therefore, more than four times as many Christians as Mohammedans in the empire.

In this fact may be seen the origin of the troubles which have given rise to the war and revolts, of which we have heard so much.

The Christians, though so much more numerous than the Turks, have been subject to them for many centuries. They have been ruled over by Turkish governors, who have sorely oppressed them, often preventing them from worshipping according to their belief, treating them with wanton cruelty, taxing them heavily and unjustly, and depriving them of many rights and privileges which their Turkish neighbors enjoyed.

The Sultan's Christian subjects, for the most part, occupy the western and northern portions of his empire. They live in Albania, Bosnia, Herzegovina, and Bulgaria; while the Servians, Montenegrins, and Roumanians, who were once subjects of the Sultan, but are now almost independent of him, are also Christians.

Most of these peoples belong to the great Sclavic race, which overran Greece before the Turks made their appearance in Europe, were converted to Christianity, and were one by one conquered and held by succeeding Sultans.

Although they have been oppressed for centuries, they have never lost their proud and fierce Sclavic spirit; and at last we see them, — first the Servians, then the Roumanians, and now the Bosnians, Bulgarians, and Herzegovinians, — rising to throw off the Turkish yoke, and to conquer their freedom.

It is true that now and then there have been long intervals when the Sultans treated their Christian subjects with mildness and justice. The great Sultan Bajazet, when he had conquered the brave Servians, ordered that, whenever a Turkish mosque was built in Servia, a Christian church should also be erected.

The recent Sultans have tried to do justice to the Christians, but they have found themselves too weak to do so. Their governors, or "pashas," have gone on oppressing and plundering them, in spite of the Sultans, who have not been strong enough to prevent these outrages.

The Christians in Turkey belong, for the most part, to the Greek Church. They have their own bishops and priests, and their churches — queer-looking structures, very low, with steep roofs, and very high, slender spires.

Many of the clergy are but poorly educated, and, as the Christians are mostly poor, hard-working shepherds, swineherds, or farmers, the priests have to work on week-days for a living, besides fulfilling their Sunday duties.

The Christians themselves, indeed, are scarcely more intelligent or enterprising than their Mohammedan fellow-subjects. Too often, in these Christian provinces of Turkey, you find bands of lawless wanderers, who pick up the best living they can by robbing and pilfering.

Unlike the Turks, who are short and swarthy, the Christians are a tall, well-formed race, with blue eyes and fair hair. They are brave and impetuous in war, and they are notable for their fondness for the music and poetry which have come down to them from the olden time, and which celebrate the period when their ancestors lived under the great and powerful Servian Empire.

"I should think," said Wyllys, "that if the Christians in Turkey outnumbered the Turks, they, with the aid of Russia, would easily overthrow the Sultan's power, even if England were to oppose such a revolution."

"But Austria also espouses the Sultan's cause."

"Why?"

"Her empire is composed of several races, who do not live very amicably together under one rule. Within her limits are Germans, Magyars or Hungarians, Czecs, and Sclaves. Each of these races distrusts the others, and fears that one of the others will gain the ascendency in the empire.

"The Austrian Sclaves border upon the Servians and Bosnians, who are also Sclaves. Austria is afraid of the latter becoming independent, or part of Russia, for then she might lose her own Sclavic population. So Austria has always sided with Turkey, and would be very likely to do so now. Besides, Austria would not like to see Russia become more powerful, and the mistress of the Lower Danube."

"How do other European nations regard the Eastern Question?" asked Wyllys.

"Neither Germany nor Italy has a direct interest in the Eastern difficulty. Their course, in case of a war, would be dictated by their alliances, and the gain they might expect from the promises of a power in return for their aid."

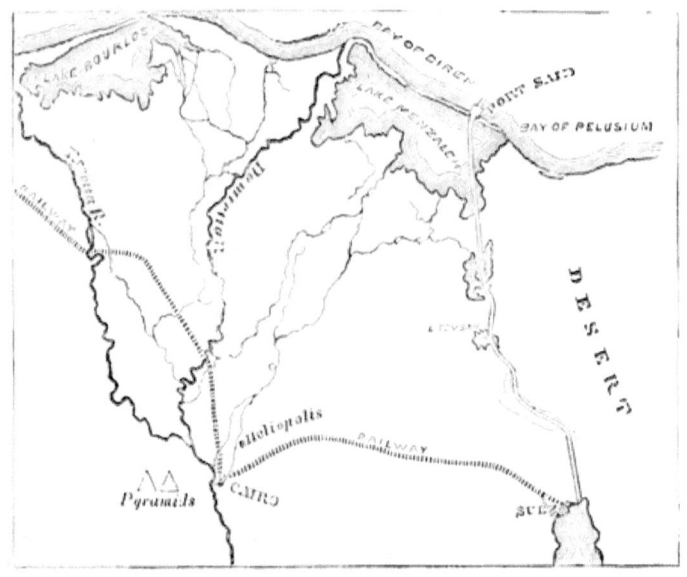

SUEZ CANAL.

"But the Suez Canal was constructed by the French, was it not? and is owned by them? It is also in Egypt?"

"Yes, but Egypt has long been a part of the Turkish Empire; but, for more than seventy years, it has been growing more and more independent of the Sultan's rule. About forty years ago the Sultan recognized Mehemet Ali as the hereditary sovereign of Egypt. Afterwards, the Egyptian ruler's title was changed from that of Viceroy to that of Khedive, or King; and a few years ago the Sultan granted him the right to conclude treaties with foreign powers, and to maintain an army and navy. Egypt still pays, however, a large annual tribute to Turkey.

"The French built the Suez Canal, but England has a greater interest in it than any other nation, as may be judged by the fact that, since it was opened, nearly three fourths of the shipping that has passed through it has carried the British flag.

"Since the canal was opened, British ships have been able to reach Bombay and other parts of India, from London or Liverpool, in a much shorter time than before. Previously, the only water-way open to British commerce was the very long, tedious, and hazardous one around the continent of Africa, by the way of the Cape of Good Hope. Now, ships leaving British ports pass directly through the Mediterranean, the Suez Canal, and the Red Sea, to their Indian destinations.

"In order to make the Suez Canal more secure to its commerce, England purchased nearly one half of the shares in the canal from the Khedive, a few years ago; that is, 176,602 shares out of a total of 400,000 shares. England may, therefore, be said to own nearly one half the canal, which is still, however, nominally under the political control and protection of the Egyptian sovereign."

"What would be the condition of affairs in Europe and the East, if the Turkish Empire were to fall?" asked Wyllys.

"Russia would probably become the great power of the Old World, and Constantinople the principal city of the Greek Church. Turkey would be a Christian empire, and Egypt would be free. Palestine would also fall under the dominion of the Eastern Church."

"Then," said Tommy, "I would just like to see Russia drive the Turks all out of Europe."

"It is probable that the Turkish Empire will, before many years, fall entirely to pieces," continued Master Lewis. "Every year it grows weaker, its debt increases, and its subjects, both in Europe and Asia, become more troublesome to govern; its condition is even now so utterly bad that no one can look for its restoration or recovery.

"Seventy years ago Turkey was extensive and powerful. The Sultan's rule extended over a large portion of Asia, and included several states in Northern Africa, and that part of Europe which lies between the Danube, the Adriatic, and the Ægean.

"One by one, provinces have revolted and become wholly or almost independent. Servia, a large state in the northwest of the empire, rebelled in 1815, and has ever since been governed by princes of her own choice. Greece, after a long and heroic struggle, of which Marco Bozzaris, so familiar to schoolboys, was one of the heroes, became free in 1830, after being subject to the Turks for three centuries. Then the two Christian provinces of Wallachia and Moldavia secured their liberty, and, uniting, became the present free principality of Roumania.

"The Sultan has also lost control of his African dominions. Egypt, Tripoli, and Tunis, though in name subject to him, are really free, having rulers of their own, and simply paying an annual tribute of money to the Sultan.

"Meanwhile the Sultan, in order to live in luxury and splendor, grinds his subjects down with heavy taxes. One tenth of all the crops raised in Turkey is paid over to the state, and the revenue thus obtained is spent, not in building roads or fostering commerce, but on the pleasures of the sovereign, and in ornamenting the capital."

"Are these the reasons why the Sultan is called the Sick Man of Turkey?" asked Tommy.

"*That* was a name given to the Sultan by the Emperor Nicholas of Russia. In conferences with the British minister in 1844, the Emperor on several occasions spoke of the Sultan as the 'Sick Man of the East.' The minutes of these conferences were laid before the British Parliament, and were published by the press, and the sobriquet thus had its origin."

"Then I understand the Eastern Question to be how to get the Turks out of Europe without disturbing the balance of the European powers," said Wyllys.

"I understand the Eastern Question to be how to keep the Turks in Europe without disturbing the balance of the European powers," said Tommy.

"There is one thing about the question I do not quite understand," said little Charlie Leland.

"What is it?" asked Mr. Beal.

"It is *how the Turks got into Europe.*"

"They gradually conquered the old Byzantine or Greek Empire. Constantine the Great became the Emperor of the world. He chose Byzantium for his capital. He became a convert to Christianity. It is said he saw, when marching at the head of his army, the figure of a cross blazing in the sky, and was thereby led to renounce heathenism. He named Byzantium Constantinople, that is, the City of Constantine. He made this city the head of the Christian Church. It afterwards became the head of the Byzantine Empire, and was renowned in arts and arms, the pride of Greece, and the glory of the East.

CONSTANTINE.

"Orkhan, a Turkish Sultan, gained a footing in Europe in the fourteenth century, by taking Gallipoli and other fortresses on the coast. Amurth, another Sultan, almost reduced the Byzantine Empire to the limits of Constantinople. Mohammed II. stormed Constantinople in 1453, and, having taken it after great slaughter, raised the crescent over the towers where had shone the cross. So Constantinople became the capital of the Ottoman Empire, and the Sultans were enthroned in the seat of the Cæsars."

"There is one thing more about the Eastern Question I do not quite understand," said Charlie.

"Well?" said Mr. Beal.

"*Who were the Turks?*"

Mr. Beal smiled.

"It is rather essential that you should know that, in order to understand the whole question, I must confess. The Christians in the Middle Ages used to pray to be 'delivered from the Turk and the devil,' and I do not wonder. The Turks were a cruel race, that inhabited the steppes near the Caspian Sea. They rapidly multiplied, and, like the Goths and Huns, began to make war their occupation. They conquered the neighboring nations by sheer barbarity, and were merciless to those who fell under their power. They gathered strength by their conquests, until they came to possess nearly all the East. The Porte became the law of Greece, Egypt, and the early nations of the world."

HUNS ON A FORAY.

"The Porte?" said Charlie.

"Yes; the gate of the Sultan's palace."

"Is the gate of the Sultan's palace the Porte?" asked Charlie.

He added, —

"I do not understand *that.*"

"Let me tell you an Eastern story," said Mr. Beal. "If you go East, Tommy," he remarked aside, "you will travel in the golden land of stories."

Mr. Beal here related the story of

THE CADI AND THE ROGUISH MOHAMMEDAN MONK.

A cadi among the Turks is the village judge. Now, a judge in any land is supposed to be a man of great wisdom and discretion, but among the Ottomans he is thought to possess almost supernatural ability. Some of the Turkish cadis certainly have exhibited very clear insight of human character, and as great tact in dealing with evil-doers.

Ayas ben Kara was a cadi who was well versed in the abstruse sciences, and who won a great reputation for discernment.

One day, as he was sitting at the gate to administer justice, a man came to him with a sorrowful face, and said, —

"I have returned from a pilgrimage to Mecca. Before I went away, I gave a purse of gold to Billah, the monk, to keep for me until my return. When I went to him and asked him for the purse to day, he denied ever having received it. What shall I do?"

"Have you spoken of this to any one?" asked the cadi.

"To no one but yourself."

"Then go. I will consider the matter. Return in three days, and I will give you my answer."

PILGRIMS TO MECCA.

The cadi sent for Billah, the monk, when he next sat at the gate.

"I am compelled," said the cadi to him, "to appoint a treasurer. I have chosen you. Here are three purses of gold that I wish to commit to your charge. God alone shall be the witness of this transaction. Your office ought to make you the most honorable of men."

"You may be certain I will be true to my trust," said the monk, greedily feasting his eyes on the purses.

"But hold," said the cadi. "I will not deliver the purses to you now, but will first inquire about your reputation. If it be good, I will send them. I am soon to make a long journey, and the treasurer whom I leave in charge of my gold must be above suspicion as well as reproach. I will see what those who have had dealings with you say of you."

The cadi dismissed the monk.

He sent for the returned pilgrim, and said,—

"Go to Billah, and demand your purse."

"But he will refuse."

"Then tell him that you will immediately lay the case before the cadi."

The pilgrim went to the monk, and said,—

"I have come again for my purse. You surely do not mean to defraud me."

"Ha! ha!" said the fat monk. "Now you see my little joke, do you? Defraud you? Not a bit! I only wished to try your temper when I refused the purse. See! here it is. I thought you would have returned for it before."

The pilgrim took his purse, and went with it to the cadi, whom he found awaiting him at the gate.

"O cadi," he said, "how shall I sufficiently praise your wisdom! Because you have led the monk to believe that he must maintain an honest reputation, he has delivered to me my gold."

A few days elapsed, the monk waiting impatiently to receive from the cadi the purses of gold.

"I will *keep* them when I get them," thought he. "I would have kept the other purse, if it had not been dangerous to my reputation, when a good name was of more value than the gold. I have lost *one* purse of gold to gain *three*. I will keep all the cadi's money so faithfully that he will never see it again, never. What a treasurer I will be!"

But the cadi's money did not arrive.

The new treasurer could wait no longer, so he went to visit the cadi, who, when he saw him coming, sat down at the gate to administer justice.

He bowed low as he came into the presence of the judge.

"Oh, you villain!" said the cadi. "Do you still think to deceive me?"

The monk was greatly astonished.

"You hypocrite!" said the judge. "A pretty treasurer you would make! I have had a view of your very soul, and seen all of its duplicity. I will publish it to the world, and you shall never get a chance to deceive the innocent any more."

ANCIENT GATE OF AN EASTERN TOWN.

The monk sneaked away with a face of shame, and the cadi warned the *faithful*, as good Mohammedans were called, never to trust him again. The people praised the cadi for his wisdom; and the poor monk suffered for his evil intentions as though he had carried out his designs. The cadi's decisions were ever received with respect, when he sat at the gate.

"That is a new kind of story," said Tommy. "I would like to hear some more like it."

"Did you notice anything peculiar about it?" asked Master Lewis. The boys were not certain.

"I will tell you one more story," said Mr. Beal.

"Perhaps you may be able to discover in it something more than a story," said Master Lewis to the boys.

MOHAMMEDAN STREET SCENE.

HOW THEY DESCRIBED A CAMEL THEY HAD NEVER SEEN.

One of the most popular of the household tales of Turkey relates to Nezar ben Maad ben Adnaan and four sons. The story illustrates the value of close habits of observation, and so it is as instructive as interesting.

Nezar ben Maad ben Adnaan had four sons, whom he named Ayaz, Mirzir, Anmaz, and Rebiah. When he was dying, he called them to him, and divided among them his property in a rather remarkable way, giving all his possessions that were *white* in color to one, all that were *black* to another, all that were *red* to the third, and his *brown* slaves to the last.

"When I am gone," said the old man, after making this remarkable will, "if there should be any difficulty arise between you, go to the Ameer Hatti Bahran, make known the same to him, and he will judge justly between you. He is one of the wisest judges that ever sat at the gate."

Not a long time after the old man's death, a disputed question arose among the four sons in regard to the will. One would suppose that it would have been easy to decide as to what was white, black, red, or brown; but avarice put strange shades on plain colors, and the dispute waxed so warm that the four sons were obliged to make a journey to the ameer, according to the provisions of the will. Now, the ameer or emir is the prince or governor of an Arabian province.

On their way, the brothers passed through a meadow, where a camel had been grazing, but which had now passed on and out of sight.

"That was a one-eyed camel," said Mirzir.

"It was laden with honey," said Ayaz. "It was also ridden by a woman."

"It was a stray camel," said Anmaz.

"It was a crooked-breasted camel," said Rebiah.

While they were thus discoursing, the owner of the camel met them.

"Have you seen a stray camel?" he asked.

"Was it a one-eyed camel?" asked Mirzir.

"Yes," answered the camel-driver.

"Was it crooked-breasted?" asked Rebiah.

"Yes."

"Had it oil on one side, honey on the other, and a woman on its back?" asked Ayaz.

"Yes," was the eager reply; "and now give me back my camel."

"We have not seen your camel," said they all.

The camel-driver grew very angry at this declaration, and accused the brothers of dealing dishonestly with him. It was agreed at last that he should accompany the brothers to the gate of the ameer, and there state his case.

"These men," said the camel-driver to the ameer, when the five had obtained an audience, "have found a camel which I lost, and they will not tell me where it is."

"How do you know that they found it?" asked the ameer.

"They correctly described it." He then related their questions when he first met them.

"We have not seen his camel," said the brothers.

"Then how could you describe it?" asked the ameer.

"I noticed that the grass where the animal had been feeding was cropped only on one side of the way," said Mirzir: "hence I thought that the animal had but one eye."

"I saw that the print of one of its forefeet was deep and the other was light," said Rebiah: "hence I inferred it was crooked-breasted."

"What sagacity and discernment!" exclaimed the ameer. "But, pray, how did you know that the camel was loaded with honey and oil, and carried a woman on its back?"

"On one side of its path," said Ayaz, "there were flies on the ground, and on the other side ants. Flies seek for honey, ants for oil. The

TRAVELLERS AND PALM-TREES.

rider in one place dismounted from her camel, and the prints of the feet were those of a woman."

The judge praised their discernment, and said to the camel-driver, —

"These are honest men. Go search for your camel."

He then asked the brothers the purpose of their coming.

They told him the story of their father's will, and of the difficulty that had arisen in regard to its interpretation.

AN EASTERN ENTERTAINMENT.

"I do not think it proper that I should interfere in a matter between persons so wise and observant as you have shown yourselves to be. But I give you a hearty welcome, and will order a feast to be spread for you."

Now the compliment of the judge to their sagacity caused all their bitter feelings to disappear, and it suddenly became easy for them to determine what things were white, black, red, and brown, and to arrive at an amicable settlement. As soon as their good humor was recovered, each was willing to speak unselfishly and make concessions; and the case showed their father's wisdom in commending them to a judge who so well understood human nature.

They were entertained at a liberal feast, which had the effect, as a good dinner usually does in such a case, of making them merry and generous-hearted. The next morning they returned in light spirits; and we hope they lived as brothers should, and did not get their colors mixed again all the rest of their lives.

When they returned they agreed that what their father had said was true.

"What was it their father said?" asked Master Lewis of the boys.

"That the ameer was one of the wisest judges that ever sat at the gate," said Wyllys. "I think I understand the meaning of the word 'Porte' now."

The other boys, however, were not as quick to see the point.

"Well, never mind to-night," said Mr. Beal. "Think upon the subject a little. Perhaps I will tell you some other Eastern stories before you go East."

ARABIAN TRAVELLERS.

CHAPTER IV.

MOHAMMEDAN WORSHIP.

Mohammedan Worship. — Mosques. — Another Strange Story. — The two little boys who were supposed to have become two little bears.

HE next evening Charlie Leland, who had become much interested in the affairs of the East, said to Master Lewis, —

"There is one point that Mr. Beal did not explain to us yesterday. What is Mohammedanism?"

"It is the belief that Mohammed was the prophet of God, and that his teachings are the true revelation of the Divine will. Mohammed was born at Mecca, about the year 570. When he was about forty years of age, he claimed that he began to receive Divine revelations. He thought angels appeared and talked with him. He once thought he was carried from Arabia to Jerusalem through the air. He wrote the Koran, gained many believers, and attempted to spread his new doctrines by the sword. He was successful in battle; and, after his death, his teachings were generally accepted in the East."

"What were his doctrines?"

"That there is no god but God, and that Mohammed is his apostle. Mohammedanism holds as sacred the Old Testament scriptures, and regards Christ as a great prophet and a wonderful revealer of Divine truth, but not equal to Mohammed. It teaches the doctrines of the immortality of the soul, the punishment of what it calls evil, and the reward of what it esteems as virtue. It pictures heaven as a place of social enjoyment. It claims that all a man's acts are preordained, and whatever happens to him is fate. The result of the Koran's doctrines

INTERIOR COURT OF A PERSIAN MOSQUE.

has been bloodshed and sensuality, and these have proved fatal to the creed. The pure teachings of Christ will live when Islamism has perished, for they are founded on holiness, and holiness is eternal truth."

DOOR OF MOSQUE OF BOU-MEDINA.

"What are the mosques?" continued Charlie.

"They are the Mohammedan houses of prayer. In their exteriors they are the most beautiful buildings in the East, and furnish the finest exhibitions of art. The interiors are inscribed with passages from the Koran, and are regarded as so sacred that the Moslem takes off his shoes when he enters. These mosques are found in nearly all parts of Asia, and in Northern Africa. The Mosque of Omar at Jerusalem is one of the most celebrated. Some of the most beautiful mosques are in India. There is a curious mosque in Semnoon, whose minaret resembles a leaning tower. The doors of mosques are often very beautiful."

The boys asked Mr. Beal to relate some more stories of the East. He told several, one of which so admirably illustrates Eastern customs that we shall give it here.

Tommy claimed to have found the meaning of *the Porte*, as the Turkish government is called.

"You repeated the word *gate* in your stories last evening," said Tommy, "because you wished

MINARET OF SEMNOON

to show that the Turkish cadis were accustomed to hold their courts in the open air at the gate of the town. The Turkish government is

GATE AT ERZEROUM.

called the Sublime Porte, because supreme law is supposed to be administered from the palace gate."

"You are right," said Master Lewis.

Mr. Beal first related the story of

THE TWO LITTLE BOYS THAT WERE SUPPOSED TO HAVE BECOME TWO LITTLE BEARS.

In the flowery land of Persia there once lived a goldsmith of great skill, and a painter of great renown. The two became as intimate as brothers, and finally each solemnly promised the other that he would be true to him in all things, and never do anything without his consent.

Having made this agreement, they started on a journey, and at last came to a convent, where they were received as guests. It was not a Mohammedan convent; but the monks placed so much confidence in the newly arrived artists as to disclose the places where they kept the golden and silver ornaments that were emblems of their faith. The artists were greedy of gain, and one night they stole all of these gold and silver images, and fled to a country of the Islamites, where they took up their abode.

Now any man who will act dishonestly towards a stranger will prove as untrue to a friend. Each of these friends, knowing that the other was wanting in principle, became jealous of the common treasure. But they agreed to put the gold and silver images into a box, and to spend only as much money, and that by mutual consent, as their necessities required.

Now the goldsmith fell in love with an amiable lady, and married her, and he found his expenses much increased. The wife bore her husband two sons, of whom he was very fond and very proud.

One day, when the painter was absent from the town, the goldsmith opened the box containing the treasures, and took one half of the gold and silver, and concealed it in his own dwelling.

When the painter returned, he discovered the theft. He questioned the goldsmith about it, but the latter denied all knowledge of the robbery, and declared his own innocence.

The painter was a shrewd man, and had a wonderful faculty of discovering secrets. He suspected the goldsmith of robbing the box, but resolved not to make his suspicions known until he should farther put them to the test.

He had two bear cubs, which he had tamed, and which he was accustomed to feed from his own hands. In his yard was also a figure made of wood, and this figure he carved and painted so that it exactly resembled the goldsmith.

He put this figure in a hidden place to which the cubs could go, and had the cubs thereafter fed by food put into the hand of the image. The cubs seemed to think that the figure was a man, and they became greatly attached to it. When hungry they would rub themselves against its legs, lick its feet, and act as a dog or cat would do in a like situation.

One day the painter invited the goldsmith and his two little boys to pay him a visit, and pass the night with him, which invitation was accepted. In the morning he took the little boys out to see his place, and shut them up in an outhouse, where their father would not be likely to find them.

"I must depart early," said the goldsmith to the painter. "Where are the boys?"

"A strange thing has happened, which has greatly astonished me, and which I hesitate to tell you, it will give you so great a shock."

"Pray, tell me at once what it is! I hope nothing has happened to the lads?"

"Indeed, there has!"

"What?"

"They have become changed!"

"How?"

"Into two little bears!"

"Impossible!"

"Yes; while they were running about, all at once each turned into a little bear! Look out of the window into the yard. There they go now!"

The people of the East are very superstitious; and a man with a guilty conscience is superstitious whether he live in the North, South, East, or West. When the goldsmith saw the two little bears, he believed the painter's word.

"Why do you think this happened?"

"I think it must have been on account of some great sin. Is their mother a good woman?"

"One of the best."

"Have you anything on your own conscience?"

"Nothing," said the goldsmith, choking.

"There they go!" said the painter; "just see them!"

The goldsmith shut his eyes at what was to him a horrible sight.

"I shall take this case to the cadi," said the goldsmith.

"I will go with you," said the painter.

The cadi heard the goldsmith's story with astonishment, and said, —

"What can this mean? Never did such a thing happen since the coming of Mohammed. What proof have you of this amazing story?"

MOSQUE AT HOOGLY

"I will bring the two little bears into court, and we will see if they will recognize their father," said the painter.

The little bears were brought into court. The painter had cunningly kept them hungry over night, and when he put them down, they ran at once to the astonished gold-

THE TWO BEARS BROUGHT INTO COURT.

smith, climbed his legs, and licked his feet, as they had been accustomed to do with the image.

The cadi was greatly affected. The goldsmith was almost beside himself with grief and pity.

"Oh, my poor little b — boys — bears —"

Not knowing whether they were boys or bears, he again reverted to the cause of the dreadful misfortune.

"I have caused all this!" he said. "I am a thief! I stole the images!"

The painter seemed greatly shocked at this confession.

"Let us take the bears home," said he, "and pray, now that you have confessed your sin, that they may be changed into boys again."

"Oh, that this might be!" said the goldsmith.

"You will put back the treasures into the box again?"

"If Allah will but pardon me."

The painter, on his return, shut up the little bears privately, and told the goldsmith to pray.

The goldsmith prayed, uttering dismal groans.

"I will go and see if your prayers have been answered," said the painter.

THE BEARS RECOGNIZING THE GOLDSMITH.

They had. The painter presently appeared, leading by the hand the two little boys.

"Allah be praised!" said the goldsmith. "My prayers are accepted!"

The astonished cadi soon summoned the painter before him, to question him in regard to these wonderful things. The painter related the true story, and was commended for his wisdom. He might have been commended by a Mohammedan cadi, but he would hardly have been praised for his artful duplicity by a Christian judge. It is not a commendable thing to practise deceit, even to gain a knowledge of the truth. But this is a rather curious story, and happily illustrates Oriental character.

After the story-telling, Master Lewis told the Class that Mr. Beal and himself had consulted together and decided upon plans for their future journeys.

"I have the permission of the parents of Wyllys and Tommy to arrange for them such journeys as I may choose," he said. "I think I will go East with them, visit Vienna, sail down the Danube, spend a few days in Constantinople, cross the Black Sea, and make a Russian journey. Mr. Beal has arranged to take the rest of the Class to Switzerland, and to return to England by the way of the Rhine. I am sorry you cannot all go East; but I can assure you that there are few things more delightful than a Swiss tour and a Rhine journey."

The boys acquiesced in the decision without any complaint, although all of them would have much preferred to make the Eastern journey.

SULTAN BAJAZET'S MOSQUE AT BROUSSA.

On the following day, Master Lewis, Wyllys, and Tommy started for Vienna, going first to Trieste. They were hurried by the locomotive past some of the fairest scenes in the world, and these were crowned with the full beauty of summer, and were flooded with the sunshine of some of the brightest days of the year. But they flew on, and all the loveliness seemed to rush backward, like dreams, into the past. Wonder succeeded wonder, and enchantment, enchantment, till the spires of Vienna glimmered before them in the rosy halos of twilight, and the curtain of night fell.

CHAPTER V.

VIENNA AND THE DANUBE.

VIENNA AND THE DANUBE. — THE ENGLISHMAN'S STORY.

T the foot of the last hills of the Wiener Wald, a chain leading up to the Alps, stands the gay capital of the Austrian Empire, full of life and beauty, and crowned with spires of art. An arm of the Danube passes round it. On the east a long plain stretches away to the dim and shadowy Carpathian Mountains. On the west are the Tyrolese Alps. The most ancient part of the city, called the Stadt, is filled with palaces and churches, museums and stately mansions. Along the borders of the Danube winds the Prater, or public park, four miles in length, and over all rises the tower of St. Stephen's, four hundred and fifty feet high, the growth of nearly one hundred years. It is a music-loving city, and the names of many great musical composers and compositions are associated with its imperial courts, its princes' liberality, and its glittering music halls. Vienna and its suburbs contain about as many inhabitants as New York, or nearly a million souls.

The Class ascended the tower of St. Stephen's, and gazed with delight on the city, the sun-flooded plain, the winding Danube, and the purple mountains. The boys were shown the stone bench, high up in the tower, from which Count Stahremberg, the brave governor of Vienna, first saw the Christian banners of Sobieski, rising above the heights of the Kahlenberg, when the noble Pole came to the rescue of the city during the siege of the Turks.

THE PRATER

"Who was Sobieski?" asked Wyllys Wynn. "I never met with his name but once before, and that was in a poem in a school-reader, —

> "'By the souls of patriots gone,
> Wake, — arise, — your fetters break,
> Kosciusco bids you on, —
> Sobieski cries, Awake!
> Rise, and front the despot czar,
> Rise, and dare the unequal war.'"

"He was a Polish patriot, who gathered a brave army, and saved Vienna from falling into the power of the Turks, in 1683."

ST. STEPHEN'S CATHEDRAL, VIENNA.

The Class spent a day in the Belvedere Palace and Museum, walking to the eminence from St. Stephen's Platz, a distance of some two miles. Here were seen the armor of emperors, kings, princes, knights,

THE BELVEDERE, VIENNA.

and even the battle-axe of Montezuma of Mexico. Here the boys were taken to the Imperial Picture Gallery, at the upper end of some beautiful gardens, and were given a catalogue, which Tommy declared it "tired his head to read."

"Just look at it!" said he in despair. "I should think it would take a lifetime to see all!— First Venetian Room, Second Venetian Room, Roman Room, Florentine School, Bolognese School, Flemish and Dutch School; *second floor*, — German School, Spanish School, and all sorts of schools, and rooms without number, and, oh, what a list of names that I never heard of! I wish I was in Constantinople, among the Turks and dogs, or at Nijni, among all the queer people! Have we to go through all of these rooms, and look at all these miles of pictures?"

"Certainly," said Wyllys. "What did we come to Vienna for? Look at the names of the old — "

"Fogies," interpolated Tommy.

"Masters," continued Wyllys sharply. "Paul Veronese, Titian, Raphael, Correggio, Vandyke, Albert Dürer, and hundreds of other great painters. This will be to me one of the rarest days of my life."

"Nearly one half of the pictures seem to be of the Virgin," said Tommy, "and no two pictures of the Virgin will be found alike. They are dreams, fancies, — all."

"But the noblest artists' conceptions of the Virgin must be a beautiful study," said Wyllys.

"Yes," said Tommy. "But look at the catalogue. First a picture of the Virgin, then one of some wicked despot, or a Cupid, Venus, — and here is one of Lucretia Borgia, — all — "

"All masterpieces of art," said Wyllys.

Tommy usually led the way in sight-seeing expeditions, but to-day he lagged behind, amid all the splendors of canvas and the glorious dreams of the old masters.

Here were pictures displaying the sufferings of Christ, and the sympathy and grief of the Holy Mother, to bring tears to the eyes; here were, as it seemed, very glimpses of Paradise, — pictures of prophets, apostles, martyrs, angels, and revelations of the Divine glory! What dreams these painters dreamed! What visions glowed before the eye of their imagination! What impresses of lofty thought blazed from these walls!

CHURCH OF ST. CHARLES BORROMEO, VIENNA.

The Class visited the Church of St. Charles Borromeo, a singular but majestic structure, of which we give a picture. It was erected by Emperor Charles VI., as a thank-offering to God for staying the great plague at Vienna.

The Class also went into the Church of the Capuchins, and descended into its vaults,— a ghostly guide, with a smoking torch, leading the way. Here were half a hundred or more metal coffins, enclosing the dust of emperors, queens, princes, and most of them bearing names of which the boys had never heard. Here was the silver coffin of

VIEW OF LINTZ.

Joseph I. Here Maria Theresa came almost every day for thirteen years to weep and pray by the remains of her husband, and here she at last was placed beside him, to share with him the silent companionship of the tomb. Here, too, is the sarcophagus of the son of Napoleon, a prince on whom once rested the hope of the French Empire, but who withered away in his youth, and received but the hollow pomps of the tombs of the Austrian emperors.

The Class made a delightful excursion, one day, a long distance up the river, to Lintz and Passau. The day had the peculiar charm of the long days of the season, breezeless and dreamy, with skies of purple and landscapes of emerald and amber fading away amid hills and forests of deeper tints and darker margins, with here and there a

MONASTERY OF MÖLK.

golden cross shining against the far shadows. Passau seemed to be a town in the river. We give a perfect picture of it, and will not describe it. Lintz presented to the river a succession of beautiful buildings under summer hills. During the excursion the Class twice passed the old Benedictine monastery of Mölk, eight hundred years old, or

VIEW OF PASSAU.

older than the first Crusade. It is an imposing-looking structure, standing on very high banks of the river.

In the Prater at Vienna, Tommy found some amusements similar to those in the parks of London, among them the performance of an elegantly dressed showman, with two dancing dogs, that quite surpassed in intelligence any dogs he had ever seen.

An act of kindness is long remembered, and he saw one in Vienna's lovely pleasure-ground that he loved to speak of to his friends. An Austrian lad, of some ten or twelve years, and evidently belonging to one of the best families, was tripping along one of the bowery avenues, with a violin under his arm. A poor boy called to him, and asked him to play. The little violinist stopped, and, tuning his instrument, struck up "The Beautiful Blue Danube." Tommy declared that the kindness of the player won his heart, and that he never had heard such beautiful music before.

DANCING DOGS.

The Danube, often spoken of in the English tongue as the "beautiful blue Danube," is not blue, but *is* one of the loveliest of rivers.

Beginning amid the mysteries of the Black Forest, it gathers volume through a course of more than seventeen hundred miles, and goes pouring over the Iron Gates at last, from which point it rolls majestically to the sea. The water is green, and is often shallow and muddy.

LITTLE VIOLINIST.

Near Vienna the river divides, and encloses the Golden Gardens, as the dreamy and romantic islands are called.

The Danube Navigation Company is one of the richest and most enterprising in the world. It controls nearly one thousand ships and tug-boats and tow-boats, of which nearly two hundred are steamers.

"The Danube has been rising from late freshets," said Master Lewis, as the Class took passage on the steamer for Pesth, the first of the excursions down the beautiful river. "I am told that this is the best time of year to sail on the river. It is neither too full and rapid, as in spring, nor too low, as later in summer."

The steamer much resembled a summer excursion boat on American rivers. It was crowded with people and merchandise. The Class was taken to the steamer by a smaller boat, for the large steamer was accustomed to start, not from the wharves, but from a point in the main stream.

The scenery was hardly interesting at the start. There were high sandbanks and willow-wooded islands, and a light mist hung over all, which gradually faded away under the brightening splendors of the sun. Here and there the river was like a calm lake or lagoon, villages appeared on the banks, the sky assumed a fixed blue color, and Nature seemed to be in a beneficent mood, and to smile on everything. A

THE DANUBE AT LINTZ.

town, called Hainburg, near which Haydn, the composer, was born, was pointed out to the Class; also a ruin, called the Castle of Theben, about which a romantic love-story is told. Presburg, in Hungary, was next passed, a city of some forty or more thousand inhabitants.

The ancient palace at Presburg stands like a castle on the hill above the town. It is said to be a mere shell, but it presents a highly picturesque appearance; and the boys will always associate it in memory with a stirring historical incident, that Master Lewis told as they were passing.

"It was in that palace," he said, "that Maria Theresa, in 1741, when surrounded by enemies, received the deputation of the Hungarian Estates. She was dressed in mourning, and wore the Hungarian

THE QUAY AND CASTLE AT PRESBURG.

Crown of St. Stephen on her head. She addressed the deputies in a powerful speech in Latin, describing the pitiful condition of her kingdom, and threw herself on their fidelity and patriotism.

"She was very beautiful then. She held her little boy in her arms, and, as she addressed the palatines, their devotion to her was renewed and kindled into enthusiasm.

"Holding out to them her child, she exclaimed, —

"'I am abandoned of my friends, pursued by my enemies, attacked

"MORIAMUR PRO REGE NOSTRO!"

by my own relatives! I have no hope but in your loyalty. I and my son here look to you for protection.'

"One of the Hungarian leaders shouted, —

"'*Moriamur pro rege nostro, Maria Theresa!*'

"The swords of the Hungarian chivalry flew out of their scabbards, and the cry was on all sides repeated, '*Moriamur pro rege nostro, Maria Theresa!*'"

The treaty of Presburg, between Napoleon and the Emperor of Austria, was signed in this city, in 1805.

The river widens just below the city, broad plains appear, and, in the distance, dark forests. Komorn next appeared, a town of some 17,000 inhabitants; then Gran, a somewhat smaller Hungarian town; then Waitzen, a town of about the size of Gran. Spires, ruins, castles, and charming estates appeared here and there; vineyards and luxuriant vegetation. Life on the banks of the Danube this sunny day seemed all like a picture or dream. The sky in the afternoon was a wide arch of illuminated purple, — deep, serene, and growing in loveliness towards evening. Near sunset, after a sail of some thirteen hours, the steamer arrived at Pesth.

The capital of Hungary is called Buda-Pesth. Buda is the old town, and is situated on the right bank of the river; Pesth is the modern city, and is built on the left bank; and a long bridge, which looks in the distance almost as slender as a spider's-web, connects the two. The city contains about 120,000 inhabitants.

The approach to Buda-Pesth by the Danube in the summer twilight furnishes an experience never to be forgotten by a lover of Nature. The city is hidden by long, low islands, covered with listless-looking trees; yet all things seem to announce that a great city is near at hand. The air is still; the sky is all violet and gold; the tide is like glass; and the water borrows beauty from the sky. The boat glides by the islands; and the Turkish city, with its quay two miles in length, with its porticos and colonnades, and its statuesque castle, surprises the eye.

"It reminds me," said Wyllys Winn, "of our approach to Edinburgh. The city wears the same appearance."

"Yes," said Master Lewis. "Pesth, at a little distance, resembles the lower part of Edinburgh; Buda reminds one of Edinburgh Castle, and the hill yonder of Arthur's Seat."

But there was no such resemblance between the two cities on a nearer view. The Class were landed at a quay filled with a gay throng.

BRIDGE AT PESTH.

There were Hungarians, Turks, Italians, and Frenchmen, loitering around the fine cafés. These saloons and dining-halls were of surprising elegance. They were richly ornamented with mirrors, fresco-painting, marble, and stucco, were connected by broad staircases, and opened into lovely courts and gardens of flowers.

The native inhabitants were a noble-looking people. Their dress

THE DANUBE AT BUDA.

was light, gay, and pleasing. The dresses of the men and women are so nearly alike that the stranger is half-persuaded that he has stumbled upon a city where all the people are males, or where all dress and look alike.

When the mists on the following morning rose, the Class beheld the Danube from the heights of Buda. On the same day the journey was renewed, and in the same dreamy atmosphere, and amid like delightful scenery, was continued towards Belgrade, the capital of Servia.

On the steamer were several passengers who spoke English. These soon made each other's acquaintance, and gathered together on the deck, and spoke of the historical associations of the scenes that they were passing.

QUAY AT PESTH.

Among these was an American lady, who had been living for some years at Innsbruck in the Tyrol. She asked Tommy what he had seen in Vienna, and gave such an interesting account of many things he might have seen, but of which he had never heard before, that he almost regretted his impatience to leave the elegant city for the East.

"Are you fond of music?" she asked. "Vienna, you know, is proud of her composers. Mozart produced his most beautiful music there. The city was the place of Haydn's triumphs. Did you visit the grave of Beethoven?"

Tommy acknowledged that he did not so much as know that Beethoven lived in Vienna.

"His life was a sad one," said the lady. "The father of Beethoven brought disgrace upon his family, and the misfortune cast a shadow over the composer's early years. His mother died when he was about seventeen years of age, leaving him poor, with two younger brothers dependent upon him for support.

"He proved himself a noble brother; but his devotion cost him many a struggle, and compelled him to make exertions far beyond his

CITADEL AT PESTH

years. At this period he played the organ in church, the viola in the orchestra, and gave instruction in music.

"His last years were embittered by the ingratitude of a nephew, who had been left an orphan, and upon whom he had lavished the rich affections of his own great heart. The youth fell into bad habits, and made an attempt to destroy his own life. By the laws of Austria the attempt was a crime, and, in this case, the offender was required to leave Vienna.

"With a forgiving love, seldom equalled, Beethoven left his home in the capital, and accompanied the exiled youth to a secluded retreat on the Danube.

"The exposure occasioned by this journey undermined the constitution of the self-sacrificing old man, and he never fully recovered from the shock.

"He died at Vienna on the evening of March 6, 1827.

"Beethoven bore all of his sorrows with fortitude; but there was one calamity that befell him that nearly crushed his spirit.

"When he had arrived at the period of what he considered to be his greatest usefulness, and when all his worldly prospects and delights seemed to depend on the single sense of hearing, he suddenly became *deaf*.

"It is enough to make one weep to read the language in which he expresses his grief in respect to this event.

"He was buried in Vienna. When you hear Beethoven's music, perhaps you may like to remember the story I have told you while gliding down the Danube."

"*I* certainly shall," said Wyllys, "and I thank you for telling it."

The scenery now had much sameness, and, to pass the time, anecdotes were told by the English-speaking travellers. Tommy repeated Mr. Beal's story of "The two Little Boys who were supposed to have become two Little Bears." The story pleased the party. An English gentleman on board seemed to enjoy the story very much indeed, and, when Tommy had concluded, he said, —

"Now I will tell a story."

THE OLD GERMAN DOCTOR WHO FELL ALL TO PIECES.

Once upon a time there lived in the city of Vienna an old German doctor, descended from a once famous Dutch family by the name of Van Tromp. He possessed wonderful wisdom and skill, and had become very rich. He was a

very sad man. He had never married, and people said that was the reason why he was so sad. He was often seen walking alone on the Prater, as the long park in Vienna is called, but never on the bright days of the public festivals, when nearly all of the people of the city throng the shadowy avenues. He was never seen at the opera, and seldom in any of the public places.

In the summer he used to leave the city quietly, sail down the Danube, and spend a few weeks at some quiet Hungarian town among the hills.

The Doctor had had a strange history. It had been his fate to be again and again disappointed in affairs of the heart. He had arranged his marriage ceremony some five times, but in each case a cruel disappointment befell him between the time of the engagement and the expected marriage. In Holland, his promised bride ran away from him with a fellow who had much brighter eyes and a prettier nose. This might have been borne, for the girl was unworthy of him. He left Holland, and went to Berlin. Here his affections revived. He courted, and thought he had won, the heart and the hand of a lovely maiden; but on the way to the church, as they were passing a regiment of returning soldiers, the girl beheld an old lover, whom she thought was dead, and she would not go with Van Tromp any further, and he returned to his lodgings very disconsolate indeed. He then went to Weimar, the Athens of Germany; and, on the banks of the Ilm, his affections again revived, and he courted another lovely creature, who, in the city of Goethe and Schiller, ought to have been very true to him. She was a peasant girl, and had been courted by a very handsome lad, who was too poor to marry. But soon after she had given her promise to Doctor Van Tromp, a fortune fell to her, and her mother came to the poor man one day to tell him that the maid had changed her mind. Then the Doctor had to resume his travels again all alone; and this time he came to Lintz on the Danube, a town famous for its beautiful women.

Here he made his fourth courtship. He offered his hand to one of the fairest of Lintz's daughters, and was accepted. One day they set out for an excursion on the Danube. The boat started just after the lady had passed on board, leaving the Doctor behind. He was a nimble jumper, and he determined to make an heroic effort to reach his bride. He leaped towards the boat, and fell into the water. When the boat returned at night, the bride did not return. The Doctor had made a frightful figure in swimming ashore, and the people on the boat had all laughed at him. But why the bride did not return to her high-jumping lover was a mystery.

"THE MAID HAD CHANGED HER MIND."

He went now down the Danube to Vienna, and here he courted a high-bred lady, the wife of an Austrian officer, who had been missing for years. He led this lady to the altar; but, just as the ceremony was about to begin, the officer appeared, and fell upon poor Doctor Van Tromp and wounded him, so that he was obliged to have one arm amputated. In his efforts to get away he also broke his leg, and a wooden one had to be substituted, all of which was very unfortunate indeed.

The Doctor was never handsome. He was too tall for a Dutchman, and was not fat enough for an attractive German. His nose was very long, and his many disappointments had caused his hair to fall off and his teeth to fall out, and his flesh to cleave very closely to his bones. But he was a man of great medical skill, and, after he had been in Vienna a few years, he was sought for by the nobility in critical cases, and he grew very rich.

In one of his summer excursions among the hills of Hungary, he met a lovely peasant girl, who lived in a cottage with an old grandmother, and his oft-blighted affections again revived. The old lady was full of aches and pains, and she found the company of the Doctor most delightful; and the young lady said she would do her best to try to love him for her poor old grandmother's sake.

The Doctor determined to make sure of a marriage this time. He had come to the conclusion that his lack of personal beauty had had much to do with his former misfortunes; and, as he was now rich, he decided he would repair himself up, and make of himself an irresistibly handsome man.

THE DOCTOR "EN DÉSHABILLÉ."

As he was a very spare man on account of his many disappointments, he provided himself with paddings and corsets, and so rounded out his form that he looked like an Austrian grand duke.

As his hair was nearly gone, especially since the last attack, he crowned himself with an immense wig, such as appears in the pictures of German virtuosos.

He procured one of the finest sets of teeth ever made in the Austrian capital.

He gloved his wooden hand, and he made up for his wooden foot by a great gold-headed cane. As his eyes had become weak from the heroic treatment of his battered body in the surgical hospital, he purchased a pair of gold-mounted goggles. He also bought an immense cloak, and on the cape of this he fastened the various diplomas and medals that his study and skill had secured to him in all the various cities of his successive disappointments.

When he went abroad now, arrayed in all these rare articles, he was indeed a wonder. Faces filled the windows and doors. The children stopped in the street, as though the grand duke were passing. The sadness passed away from his face; hope lighted it up with smiles again, and smoothed out the wrinkles. What would have said his four faithless brides could they have seen him now!

He determined, as I said, to make a sure marriage this time. When he went to propose to the pretty and dutiful Hungarian maiden, he asked, —

"Have you a lover?"

"No."

"Did you ever fall in love before?"

"No; I never was in love."

"Have you been acquainted with any soldiers?"

"No."

"You have no relations to leave you a fortune?"

"No."

"Then," thought the Doctor, "I have only not to take the maiden away from her home before the wedding-day, so that no such accident as the boat and wharf unexpectedly parting happen, and I am sure of a modest little wife to share with me my fortune and glory. I will take the bride and her grandmother to Vienna, and I will spend my last years amid the delights of a loving home."

The wedding-day was appointed. The house in Vienna was furnished. The maiden had invited the simple Hungarian peasants of her acquaintance to attend the ceremony, and receive her parting expressions of affection.

So, one morning in early autumn, the Doctor, arrayed in his paddings, his wig, his wooden arm and leg, his dentistry, his goggles, his cloak, his medals, and his cane, left Vienna, and, taking the boat down the Danube, landed at the little Hungarian town.

It was nearly evening, and, full of blissful anticipation, he set out for the bride's house, taking a somewhat secluded path over the hills.

Now in that country there were *bears*.

As the Doctor walked over the hills, he tried to sing. How blessings brighten as they are about to fly! It was a pretty German song he began to sing; perhaps it was associated with his former sad experiences, —

> "How can I leave thee,
> Queen of my loving heart,
> Dearer to me thou art
> Than aught beside."

The sun was sinking in a sky all purple and amber, and the shade of night was slowly creeping over the eastern hills.

Now, a bear on a near hill-side heard the singing, and, seeing a curious figure plodding along, stood up on its haunches to hear and see what must have appeared to him a prodigy. He doubtless viewed the Doctor much as the boy looks upon the elephant when the menagerie passes. The big wig, the flying cloak, the heavy cane, and the echoing song evidently excited Bruin's curiosity; and, when the Doctor had sailed by full of happiness, the bear came out of the wood into the road, and trotted along behind him. Whether or not he had any evil intent, I cannot tell; perhaps he was lonesome, and wanted company.

THE DOCTOR FOLLOWED BY THE BEAR.

Presently the Doctor, in the midst of the pretty German melody, heard the pat of feet behind him, and looked around. His song ceased very suddenly, or, rather, ended in some very wild German adjectives, of which we have no translation, as we have of the song.

He lifted his cane with staring eyes.

He flapped his great cloak and all of its medals, like wings.

Bruin appeared very much astonished. He stopped, and stood up again on his haunches.

The Doctor exclaimed,—

"The Fates are adamant!"

He started to run.

He lost his gold-mounted goggles.

Bruin ran, too,—after the Doctor.

So the Doctor did not stop to pick up his goggles. He would have picked up a live coal as soon.

His wig caught in one of the branches of the forest trees. The Doctor looked around, and caught another glimpse of Bruin, and he did not stop to recover his wig. He only said,—

"The Fates are brass!"

And while struggling up the hill, he felt his stays unlace.

"Now I am undone!" he exclaimed. "It seems as though the Fates are iron!"

As he reached the top of the hill, a high wind struck him. His

THE DOCTOR CHASED BY THE BEAR.

teeth began to chatter, and presently dropped out, and then his cloak, with its medals, was lifted into the air, and went flying to some unknown place.

But the cottage of the bride was now in sight before him. Oh, place of refuge! The bear was also in sight behind him! Oh, dreadful apparition! The bear had until now waddled along in an uncertain way, but he suddenly quickened his pace. So did the Doctor; he flew, bounding up and down.

The bride now came to the door, expecting to see the bridegroom. She saw a spectral-looking object approaching, followed by the bear.

She closed and barred the door.

"Look out, granny," she said, "and tell me what you see."

"Bad luck, bad luck to ye, my daughter, and bad luck to us all! It is a wizard!"

Presently the door was shaken, filling the bride and wedding guests with terror. The old crone sat wringing her hands, and crying, "Bad luck, bad luck to us all! It is the fiend!"

Presently a sound was heard upon the roof, then in the chamber, and soon a

fearful-looking object, without hair or teeth, with only one arm, with one foot twisted around, and with humps all about him, descended the stair, and exclaimed,

"I have come!"

"Who are you?" cried the affrighted bride.

"I am your lover! I have come to be married!"

"You have deceived me!" said the bride. "You are not the man who courted me!"

"He has been transformed by some bad spirit!" said the old woman.

CASTLE ON THE DANUBE.

"Where's your hair, and teeth, and arm, and leg, and other parts of your body?"

"I do declare," said the Doctor, "I have left myself all along the way, and have fallen all to pieces!"

"And there is not enough left of you to make a bridegroom for my daughter's daughter. I pray you, begone!"

Then the peasants accompanied the sorrowful Doctor back to the little town on the Danube, and the next day he returned to Vienna, believing that Fate intended him for a single life, and resolving to struggle against his destiny no more.

The boat glided along on the breezeless river. In the afternoon a tributary river, called the Drave, was passed. The Danube then grew darker in color, and seemed to run more swiftly. Dusky woods covered the hills, and in several places picturesque ruins appeared. The sky was violet, with a rosy tint near sunset. The twilight was a lingering splendor, followed by the rising of the moon over the quiet hills. In one place the moon shone through a ruin of a church or castle.

"I have seen views like that in pictures," said Tommy; "but I supposed such scenes were only painters' fancies."

The English people asked the lady from Tyrol to sing.

"What would you like to hear?" she asked.

"'*Do you recall that night in June, upon the Danube River?*'" suggested Wyllys.

"I will sing a ballad of the Tyrol," said the lady, "and you, perhaps, will favor us with the song you name. *That* is not familiar to me."

It was a glorious night, like dreamland; and, listening to singing and to incidents of travel, the Class at last reached the borders of the East, — Belgrade.

CHAPTER VI.

THE CRUSADES.

Through Servia. — The Crusades. — The Story of the Puzzled Executors.

HE blood that has flowed at Belgrade would indeed redden the Danube, from the heroic land of which it is the capital and entrepôt to the Black Sea. The place was styled by the Turks "The House of the Holy War." We will not stop here to recount its history, sieges and slaughters, slaughters and sieges. This is the story in a word, — the soil is full of the bones of Turk and Christian. It is said that a comet once filled the sky before one of these periodical drenchings of the soil in blood; and, if ever there was a place where it would seem portents might have been seen, it was here. It is a town of about 26,000 inhabitants, and the hotel accommodations for travellers are good. The summer sun shines on the peaceful-looking fortress, and the moon mirrors herself in the Danube, all as beautifully as though death did not hide its doings everywhere in the soil.

"It was over the way that we have been travelling," said Master Lewis, at Belgrade one evening, to the boys, "that the Crusaders swept. Their principal route was by the countries of Germany, Hungary, and Bulgaria, to Constantinople, and the Danube afforded them one of the fairest scenes on their march. The Greek or Eastern Empire was in its glory then, and Constantinople was the Queen City of the Church. It seemed at one time as though the kingdoms of the Western World were marching to the East to recover the sepulchre of the Lord. One historian claims that as many as 6,000,000, in the spring of 1096, were on their way towards Palestine. There was but one thought in France, England, Germany, and the lands of the North, and that was the Crusade."

"Do you think the army was as large as that?" asked Wyllys.

"No," said Master Lewis. "I was about to greatly modify the

CITY OF BELGRADE.

statement. But the army numbered hundreds of thousands, and it was over the lands we have been seeing, and are to see, that it marched, glowing with hope and confident of victory."

"Were the Crusaders not victorious?" asked Tommy.

"For a time: the first great Crusade ended in victory. Let me tell you

THE STORY OF THE VICTORIOUS CRUSADE.

To go to Jerusalem, to visit the Mount of Olives, Calvary, and the tomb of Jesus, became one of the passions of the Christians of Europe, in the early age of the Church. Under Constantine, as I have told you, Christianity arose from the cross to wear the crown of the world. Temples and churches covered the holy places of Jerusalem, Bethlehem, and Nazareth. The pilgrims increased in

FORTRESS OF BELGRADE.

number, and at last St. Helena, the mother of Constantine, at the age of seventy-eight, visited the holy places, and discovered what was supposed to be the wood of the true cross.

St. Jerome, from his retreat in Bethlehem, once wrote an account of the coming of these bands of pilgrims.

In a letter to St. Paulinus, he uttered these truthful and sensible words, —
"The court of heaven is as open in Britain as at Jerusalem."

It would seem that readers of the Bible would have learned this truth from the words of Christ to the woman of Samaria. But they did not.

Palestine became conquered by the Moslems, who mercilessly slaughtered the bands of Christian pilgrims wherever they found them.

Then rose Peter the Hermit, of Amiens, France, and preached the duty of all Christians uniting in a crusade to recover Jerusalem. A great council of Christian leaders was held at Clermont in France. Pope Urban II. was there, thirteen archbishops, and more than two hundred bishops. People flocked to the place in multitudes, — princes, grandees, knights. The church could not hold them. A pavilion was erected out of doors for the speakers, and on a high platform Peter and the Pope took their stand, and the fiery-minded Urban addressed

CRUSADERS ON THEIR WAY.

the multitude. He appealed to the national pride of France, and alluded to the virtues and greatness of Charlemagne.

"It is from you," he said, "above all nations, that Jerusalem awaits the help she invokes. Take ye, then, the road to Jerusalem, assured of the imperishable glory which awaits you in the kingdom of heaven."

"*Deus vult!*" (God willeth it), cried the multitude on every hand.

"If the Lord God were not in your souls," said the Pope, "ye would not have uttered the same words. In the battle, then, be those words your war-cry, — those words that came from God ; in the army of the Lord let naught be heard but that one shout, '*God willeth it ! God willeth it !*'"

It seems strange that such a delusion could have filled the souls of students of the New Testament; for Christ plainly taught that the warfare of his kingdom was to be a spiritual contest with sin, and that those who take the sword shall perish with the sword.

Thousands upon thousands of people hurried to the call of Urban, to engage in the Holy War. The first division of the Crusaders marched through Hungary, and were cut to pieces in Bulgaria. The second, under Peter the Hermit, reached Constantinople, crossed the Bosphorus, and were defeated by the Turks at Nice. Then came a great army, led by Christian princes, of whom I told you when we were in England and France. There were at least 600,000 soldiers in this army, and a great retinue of followers beside. Thousands perished of sickness and fatigue on the long and perilous way. After a seven-months' siege, the princes captured Antioch, in June, 1098. Again a terrible battle was fought, and another triumph won. The way to Jerusalem now opened.

On a bright summer morning in 1099, 40,000 Crusaders, all that were left of the vast army that had left the West two years before, marched towards Jerusalem.

ALLEGORICAL PICTURE OF CHARLEMAGNE.

Over every hill-top as they went, they strained their eyes to catch a glimpse of the Holy City. At last the city appeared: from the heights of Emmaus, on June 10, 1099, they saw it; it was a thrilling moment, and the joy was so great that the army of men wept like children.

The city was taken after a siege, and Godfrey of Bouillon was made King of Jerusalem. So triumphantly ended the First Crusade.

It had been Master Lewis's plan to go down the Danube to Rustchuk, and there take the train for Varna, and proceed from Varna by steamer to Constantinople, by way of the Black Sea and the Bosphorus. But he met a party of traders at Belgrade, among whom was the Englishman of whom we have spoken and an English-speaking Jew, who were about to visit several towns in the interior of Servia; and a rare opportunity was thus offered the Class to see a part of Turkey not often visited by tourists.

The preparations for this journey were somewhat peculiar, and much amused Tommy. Kettles, carpets on which to sleep, wide pairs

CRUSADERS PERISHING BY THE WAY.

of Turkish trousers in which to ride when travelling on horseback, baggage horses, and a grotesque-looking Tartar guide, all made the party quite resemble a band of gypsies on one of their wanderings.

The party started for Novi Bazaar. The distance as the bird flies would hardly seem to be more than one hundred and fifty miles, but the zigzag road that was followed made the journey a very long one. The first stage of it was to Kragushevatz, the former capital of Servia;

the second to Krushevatz; the third a zigzag through Central Servia; and the fourth to Novi Bazaar.

The Class was surprised to find in this Turkish country a landscape very similar to England. The vegetation was nearly the same. The sides of the road were often carpeted with the wild strawberry, and the open glades, which ran into the woods, abounded with the raspberry. Bushes covered the sides of the hills; and when Tommy found that these bore the whortleberry, he said he felt as though he "was in the neighborhood of home." The flowers, too, were like those of England and America. The hedges were clothed with the honeysuckle and clematis.

The Servian cottage, too, reminded the Class of the low cottages in the South of England,

WAYSIDE SHRINE IN THE EAST.

and of pictures of the log-houses in the West in America. They stood in the midst of small orchards of cherry, plum, apple, and pear trees, and often one reminded the tourist of some "old house at home."

The party started for the interior from Semandria, on the Danube, below Belgrade. The road taken at first was the great highway to

Constantinople that sweeps down through Hungary, and crosses the Danube at Belgrade, follows the river to Semandria, and the river Morava far into the interior.

The suburbs of Belgrade, in the direction of the interior, are interesting. The cottages of logs or of cob, with thatched roofs and enormous chimneys, have a look of homely thrift and comfort, as have their green surroundings. Market women, with yellow kerchiefs on their heads, gypsy women, with Egyptian-looking faces and Theban-like dress, were met in the morning as the travellers went out of the city. One of the ambitions of the Servian peasant woman is to decorate her head and neck with coins. The Class met many of these fair peasants, on the road from Belgrade, whose faces were not their only fortunes. Tommy said the girls looked as attractive as "savings banks," and that to marry a number of them would be to possess a fortune.

THE VICTORIOUS CRUSADE.

The situation of Semandria is picturesque, at the foot of a range of hills, some of which overhang it. It is semicircled with cottages with green gardens. The old fortress that commands the Danube looks like

SERVIAN PEASANTS.

a coronet, with its regular succession of square towers. The oldest church in Servia, according to tradition, is here. It is found on one of the spurs of a range of hills, which rise like a half-moon to the west and south of the town. It is built against a high bank, and the floor is some six or seven feet below the surface of the ground on the outside. It looks as though it had been dug out of the hill.

The tradition is that this church was once *buried* to hide it from

SERVIAN HEAD-DRESSES.

the Turks. If the story be true, the structure is one of the most curious in the world. It is called the Chapel of St. Mary. It is only thirty-eight feet long. A cemetery surrounds it.

The journey to Novi Bazaar occupied nearly a week. The Class was quartered at night in towns of unpronounceable names, and whose spelling seems to differ with every map. In several of these inns, if inns they could be called, the furniture of the room consisted of the floor, and on this the boys spread their blankets and slept. Their sleep was sound; after the long rides they were grateful for even a floor to lie upon.

The scenes by the way were pleasing. Servia contains more than a million people; among these are some 25,000 gypsies.

Again and again these bands of forest people were seen in bowery places, near which was pasturage for their ponies. In some places they were discovered in green huts, which they had built of boughs to shelter them from the sun.

PRIEST OF THE GREEK CHURCH.

The Servians are a noble race, — heroic, susceptible to sentiment and beauty, fond of bright costumes, poetry, and music. They belong to the Greek Church, and have some three hundred churches and more than six hundred parishes and six hundred ministers. Education, of course, is not neglected among a people of such cultivated taste. There are more than three hundred educational institutions in Servia.

The Servians are a polite people. The Class frequently met groups of peasants, going to and returning from their labor in the fields. As soon as these saw the travellers, they stopped respectfully and waited for them to pass. They seemed to regard it as ill-bred to cross a road in front of a traveller. Their attachment to their friends is strong, and they give expression to it in ways seldom seen in English-speaking countries. In one town where the Class stopped, if a collection of rude huts could be called a town, a man returned home who had been long absent. He was embraced and kissed by his old companions, from gray-haired farmers to boys in their teens. All of the children kissed his hands. It was a touching sight, and showed that the affections of the heart are the same in all lands.

During a part of the journey the party was accompanied by a young Servian, who happened to be travelling in the same direction. His costume was peculiar, but very graceful and rather becoming. It abounded in bright colors. On his head he wore a cap of *red* cloth, with a *black* silk tassel; his collar-tie was *magenta* and *white*; his shirt-front was embroidered; his vest was *blue*; his jacket was *purple*, and was lined with fur, although it was midsummer; his girdle was of *red* leather, and over it was a sash of silk and *gold*; his trousers were *purple*, his garters *red*, and his stockings *red* and *black*. These colors were jauntily arranged, with a view to picturesque effect. He was very handsome and lively, and seemed to have a warm, generous nature; and the travellers felt that they had lost a friend when he left them.

All along the way in the pastures were places where had been great fires. Tommy asked the meaning of this, and received an unexpected explanation from the English-speaking Jew in the party, who was somewhat acquainted with the country.

"From April until June," he said, "the valleys of Servia are infested by a small fly, the *Simulium reptans*. It attacks the nostrils of cattle, and causes almost immediate death, it is so poisonous. This fly cannot endure smoke; hence fires are kept burning in the pastures."

The fat Englishman, who had related the story of the German doctor that fell all to pieces, was the most interesting member of the party. His conversations by the way with the Hungarian Jew, who spoke English, were often both instructive and entertaining to the Class. One of these was about the mysterious fate of the late Sultan Abdul Aziz.

"Pride turned his head," said the Jew; "and, when he saw his power departing, he went mad and killed himself."

"It was Fate," said the Tartar guide, a true Mohammedan.

"How did he kill himself?" asked Tommy of the fat Englishman.

"I do not know. No one seems to understand the exact facts of the case. Many people believe he was assassinated by the Softas."

"Who are the Softas?" asked Tommy.

"They are Mohammedan students, who are sworn to maintain their faith."

GEORGE III.

"You said that Abdul Aziz became insane," continued Tommy, referring to the remark of the Jew. "I should think an insane despot would be a dangerous man indeed."

THOU ART BETRAYED!

"King Theodore was a dangerous man, a very dangerous man," said the Jew. "But insane monarchs have not been confined to the East. George III. was insane in his middle life and last years."

"And Charles VI. of France," said the Englishman. "When I am riding through a strange wood, as we are now, and I happen to be left behind my party, I often think of Charles's warning, which drove him insane."

"Relate the story," said Tommy.

And in the woods of Servia, the Englishman, assisted by Master Lewis, told the story of poor Charles VI.: How, on one blazing day in August, 1392, he was travelling in the forest of Le Mans, when there glided from behind a tree a tall man, with bare head and feet, clad in a white smock, and seized his horse by the bridle; how this strange man shrieked, "Thou art betrayed!" how he followed the king, crying the dreadful words, and then glided away into the forest again; and from that moment the king believed there were traitors on every hand, went mad, and had to be bound. This is not an Eastern story, or we would tell it in full here. It can be found in the history of France.

The Jew was a singer, and sang several lively Hungarian and Servian songs, in different parts of the journey. One of these ballads began as follows:—

> "The Magyar maid alone should be
> The wife of Magyar man,
> For she can cook, and only she,
> Our soup of red cayenne."

At one of the villages where the party stopped, soup was served to the travellers.

"Here we have a luxury," said the Jew; "here is the dish of which Hungarians and Servians love to sing."

"The Magyar maid's soup," said Wyllys.

The Jew swallowed his portion with evident relish. The fat Englishman tasted cautiously and began to shed tears. Tommy took a large mouthful of the fiery compound, with electrical effect. He covered his face quickly with his hands; then sat in silence, pressing his nose and face with great force, and perhaps thinking of the Magyar maid.

"How do you feel?" asked the Englishman, after observing Tommy's odd movements.

"Just as though I had swallowed a bumble-bee," said Tommy, taking down his hands for a moment, but resuming his former attitude.

He did not take any more of the Magyar-maid soup.

"You won't go back to get a wife among the Magyar maids?" said the Englishman ironically.

"No," said Tommy, "not if she makes such soup as that."

"The poetic flavor is rather high," added the good-humored traveller.

"I should think such soup as that would inspire a poet to sing," said Tommy. "It would have made me sing, if I had dared to take breath."

The summer journey through Servia was on the whole delightful, though at times the heat was intense. The mountainous borders of Bosnia were at length reached, and the party soon entered Novi Bazaar.

The Class had expected to find an Oriental city of fortresses, mosques, churches, palaces, parks, and gardens. But no such scene of Eastern splendor appeared. Novi Bazaar is indeed what its name implies, — a new trades town. It is situated at the crossing of the great roads of the country, has some 15,000 inhabitants, and is a place of great fairs. Many of the houses are built of mud. The people seemed less hospitable than the Servians of the Danube, but were lively and cheerful. The Class were entertained on the evening of their arrival by the graceful dancing of a beautiful Bosnian girl.

The Class made a single excursion from the town, and on this the dark peaks of Montenegro were seen, and a party of Montenegrins was met.

Master Lewis would have been glad to visit Montenegro, but it is best approached by way of the sea and Austria. Through fear of invasion, the Montenegrins did not, until recently, allow the construction of roads. The ways into the principality through the mountain passes are chiefly foot-paths.

Master Lewis, however, did not fail to relate to the Class many facts and incidents concerning the heroic principality, whose mountain-tops were already in sight, and some of whose people he was proud to meet. After his excursion into Bosnia, by the old European highway that runs almost under the dark shadows of the Montenegrin hills, he seemed to have visited the place, and we will give in another chapter his account of Montenegro to the Class, and a romantic story that he told.

The Class took leave of the party with whom it had travelled through Servia at Novi Bazaar. Tommy was sorry to part with his corpulent English friend, who had told him many stories and played upon him some pleasant jokes.

Among the stories that the Englishman related was one that Tommy liked to repeat; and he sent his own version of it to Mr. Beal in Germany, and asked that gentleman to read it to the Class under his charge.

THE PUZZLED EXECUTOR.

There was a Turkish gentleman whose property consisted of seventeen valuable horses. The beauty of the animals made him both rich and famous. His stables were visited by princes. There were no horses like his.

He was taken suddenly ill. The doctor gave him no hope, and, in much confusion of mind, he made his will.

He had three sons.

To the first he gave one half of his seventeen horses.
To the second he gave one third of his seventeen horses.
To the third he gave one ninth of his seventeen horses.
And he died.

After his funeral, his executor called together the three sons to divide among them the horses.

"Seventeen," he said, "will not divide by two, nor by three, nor by nine. I wish to be just. What am I to do?"

The sons could not answer.

While the question was puzzling the brains of the four, a dervish came riding that way. The sons proposed submitting the question to him.

Now a dervish is a Turkish monk, who lives in poverty, and is supposed to be very pious, wise, and just.

He heard the case, and considered it, and at last said, —

"Take my horse, and add him to the others, then you will have eighteen."

The executor now made the division.

He gave the first son one half of the horses, — *nine*.

The second one third of the horses, — *six*.

The third one ninth, — *two*.

In all, —*seventeen*.

The dervish then said, —

"You will not need my horse, since you have an equal division. I will take him back again."

And the dervish rode away.

The sons rejoiced that there was such a wise man abroad, and all were happy.

MONTENEGRINS.

CHAPTER VII.

THE STORY OF MONTENEGRO.

THE STORY OF MONTENEGRO AND A STORY OF MONTENEGRO.

HIS is a little principality of Turkey, the independent spirit and heroism of whose people have won the admiration of the world. It contains about 130,000 inhabitants.

It resembles the White and Franconia Mountain region in New Hampshire, only its principal peaks are higher than Mt. Washington, of the White Mountains, and Mt. Lafayette, of the Franconia range. The whole of New Hampshire comprises about 9,280 square miles. This little principality has about 1,680 square miles. It is nearly sixty miles long and thirty-five broad. It lies south of Servia, near the Adriatic Sea. It is separated from the Adriatic by a narrow strip of land belonging to Austria.

It is called Montenegro, or Black Mountain, on account of the dark color of its hills and peaks. One of its peaks is nearly 10,000 feet high. Mt. Washington, in New Hampshire, is a little more than 6,000 feet high.

The mountains of Montenegro are covered with dark forests of fir, ash, beech, oak, ilex, willow, and poplar. It is a beautiful region, full of noble scenery.

It is a healthy territory, and the people are famous for their simple manners and vigorous constitution and resolute character.

In 1476, when the Byzantine Empire and the Greek Church were falling on all sides before the power of the conquering Turk, Montenegro resolved that she would never surrender her liberty.

AMONG THE PEAKS.

A queer law was enacted at this time. It was that if any Montenegrin should ever, in war, turn his back to the Turk, he should be dressed

MONTENEGRIN CAVALRY.

in a woman's clothes, be whipped by the women, and then sent beyond the territory never to return. The Turks have never been able to subdue Montenegro.

Small as she is, with a capital which is only a village with a single street, and an army of but twenty thousand men, Montenegro has for centuries stoutly maintained her independence, and proved herself unconquerable. The brave people, from the mountain fastnesses, have defied the Turks and all their enemies.

The Montenegrins belong to the Servian race, which once formed a great empire in that region. The men are described as tall and squarely built, with long brown hair and dark-blue eyes, and with faces beaming with intelligence. The women are of a medium height, with thick-set bodies and dark countenances. They are cheerful looking, but inferior in intelligence to the men.

The present Prince of Montenegro, who himself commanded his troops against the Turks in the late war, is a fine, manly person, — tall, dark, and handsome. He is brave and enterprising, and takes a keen interest in the making of highways, and in the progress of education among his subjects.

Both the dress and the customs of the Montenegrins are quaint and romantic. The attire of the people is brilliant in its variety of color. They wear long white coats, red waistcoats, blue trousers reaching to the knee, and white gaiters; their caps are round and flat, and are worked in gold embroidery.

It is an illustration of the simplicity of the government that, at Cettinje, the capital, one may sometimes see the prince and his Senate sitting in the open air, on a green near the prince's humble palace, administering justice. The prince does not keep up a very splendid state; for the income of the principality is only about fifty thousand dollars a year, and his residence is not half so luxurious as are those of the well-to-do citizens of an American city.

Many years ago, or in the fifteenth century, there lived in Montenegro a heroic prince, called Ivan Bey. His true name was Ivan Beyova.

Venice was in her glory then, — beautiful Venice, which filled a hundred islands with palaces, just across the calm, blue sea.

In 1483, Ivan Bey went to Venice, and sought a wife for each of his sons. Now, Ivan was proud of the beauty of the young men of his mountain land, and he thought his son Stanicha one of the handsomest young men in the world.

MONTENEGRIN BOY.

He sought the hand of the daughter of the Doge for Stanicha. He said to the Doge a very pretty thing, according to the historic ballads, —

"Hearken to me, Doge! Thou hast in thy house the most beautiful of roses, and there is in my house the handsomest of pinks. Doge, let us unite the rose and pink."

It is well for a man to think well of his children.

Ivan went to Venice, taking to the glittering city three loads of gold. He gained the promise of the maiden's hand for his son, and it was agreed that the wedding should take place at the next vintage.

He was about to depart, highly delighted with his success, when he said to the Doge, —

MONTENEGRIN SENATOR.

"Friend, thou shalt soon see me again, with six hundred men from across the Gulf. If there be among them a single one who is handsomer than my own son Stanicha, you may give me neither bride nor dower."

Soon after the happy Ivan returned to his mountains, the handsome Stanicha fell sick (of all the diseases in the world) of small-pox. When

BLACK MOUNTAINS.

he recovered, his beauty had gone; he was one of the homeliest young men ever seen in the land.

The autumn came, and Ivan grew very sad. He could not take such a disfigured son to such a bride.

Now Ivan's wife was a very sensible woman, and, when she discovered what made her husband so sad, she said to him, —

"It serves you right! It is a punishment for your pride! You, as an orthodox Christian, ought not to have sought the hand of a Latin lady for our son."

A long time passed. At length there came sailing across the sunny Adriatic a fine ship, bearing a message from the Doge. It was a very delicate one, — quite a little poem, if we may accept the ballad as true. It said, —

"When thou enclosest a meadow with hedges, thou mowest it, or thou leavest it to another, that the snows of winter may not spoil the flourishing grass."

This was quite a riddle. We think the reader can guess its meaning. It was like saying, When one asks a bride, and obtains her, one should come for her, or else free her from her engagement.

Ivan assembled six hundred Servians, the handsomest of the race.

"I am going to Venice," he said, "to secure the daughter of the Doge for my son. I cannot take my son with me, because I have promised the Doge the handsomest man in Servia for his daughter. Choose me a man to represent him. Which is the fairest of you all?"

There was a young man of noble family, named Obsenovo Djuro, who was noble in mien and perfect in features, and the assembly pointed to him.

"You shall represent my son," said Ivan. "I shall cause the Doge to believe that you are my son. Act well your part, and you shall receive half of the presents that the Doge bestows."

Djuro was very unwilling to play a part like this. He felt it unworthy of his religion and manhood. But he obeyed.

The Doge received Ivan with great pomp. He gave a feast to the six hundred youths that lasted a week. The ducal palace was filled with music by day, and its gemmed walls were a blaze of light at night.

Then Ivan said, —

"We must back to the mountains. Bring to us the bride."

The Doge said, —

"Which of the young men is Stanicha?"

The Servians pointed to Djuro.

The Doge gave Djuro the kiss and the golden apple. Now, the golden apple was the choicest marriage gift.

The sons of the Doge came forward, loaded with presents of gold. They asked, —

A MONTENEGRIN SOLDIER.

"Where is Stanicha?"

The Servians pointed to Djuro.

They embraced him, and gave him garments of gold.

The Doge's family came, and asked for Stanicha.

The Servians pointed to Djuro.

The household enriched him with gifts, and the bridal party returned to Servia.

When the bride arrived in Servia, she was told the story of the strategem, and was asked to accept the withered and repulsive princelet. She pitied his misfortunes, and yielded to the situation in a generous and noble spirit. But when Djuro claimed half the bridal presents, her pride was touched, and she resisted the payment of the claim

"You must maintain my cause," she said to Stanicha, "if it has to be done by the sword. Else I will take my courser, and turn to the shore, and my falcon shall bear the story of my wrongs to the Doge."

MONTENEGRIN GIRL

Stanicha was greatly vexed that Djuro should press the claim. He sought him, met him at the foot of a dark mountain, and there slew him with his own hand.

The Servians heard of the deed with horror; they loved Djuro, and resolved to avenge his death.

Stanicha fled to Constantinople. He embraced Islamism, raised a Turkish army, and tried to recover the principality. But he was defeated, and died in disgrace. His children founded noble families in Albania, and their descendants held a certain rank until 1833, when the last of the known family of Ivan Bey was exiled by the Porte.

"I would like to visit Montenegro," said Tommy.

"It would not be easy to do so," said Master Lewis, "except by the way of the Adriatic. The paths are dangerous and difficult, and we would find ourselves entirely among strangers, dependent on the private hospitality of a people whose language we cannot speak, and who would naturally regard us with suspicion. Besides, we have not the time for long horseback journeys."

BULGARIAN TRAMPS.

CHAPTER VIII.

BULGARIA AND THE DARDANELLES.

BULGARIA. — THE DARDANELLES. — A TURKISH ROMANCE. — THE OLD WOMAN WHO
COULD TEACH TRICKS TO A FOX.

N leaving Novi Bazaar, the Class journeyed to Mitrovitsa, whence the new route by rail to Salonica, thus passing through the new boundaries of Bulgaria, on the way to the sea.

We have heard a great deal of the cruelties which the Turks, a few years ago, visited upon thousands of the Bulgarians, — terrible stories of whole families murdered, of tortures inflicted upon innocent babes, and of villages left solitary and desolate by their fleeing inhabitants.

These atrocities have occurred because the poor Bulgarians tried to free themselves from the tyranny and debasing rule of the Sultan; but many of those who suffered from them were innocent even of this offence.

Who are these Bulgarians, and what sort of people are they? If you will look on the map of Turkey in Europe, you will see that Bulgaria is a long, narrow, irregular district, lying between the river Danube on the north, and the lofty and picturesque Balkan mountain range on the south; while on the west it borders on Servia, and on the east is washed by the waves of the Black Sea.

You will observe that it is hilly in places; and that in every direction winding rivers flow through its territory.

It is a beautiful and productive land, — this Bulgaria. Broad, fertile plains rise gradually from the Danube to the mountains, and slope down to the shores of the Black Sea. Nature has blessed it; and it is too fair a country to be the sad scene of havoc and bloodshed.

The Bulgarians are a simple, ignorant, good-humored, industrious, and submissive race. They are slow and stolid, and strongly attached to their homes and their farms. They could be easily governed, if their Turkish rulers would only treat them kindly and let them pursue their labor and lives in peace.

They are a very mixed people. Of the whole population, about a million and a half are Bulgarians, and half a million are Turks. Besides these, in Eastern Bulgaria about one hundred thousand Tartars dwell; while nearly as many Circassians, who have wandered thither from beyond the Black Sea, are settled among the mountains and hills in the west.

In passing through Bulgaria, you find many wandering tribes of gypsies, with queer dresses, and hats decked off with many colored ribbons; while in the towns you see, at every turn, the strongly marked features of the Jews who have gathered in them.

The descendants of the old Bulgarian race are called "rayahs." They are for the most part farmers and shepherds, while in the towns they are mechanics.

The Bulgarian villages are very curious and peculiar to the eyes of a stranger. Each consists of some thirty or forty huts clustered together, which are plastered with mud. Around each house is usually a high, singularly built fence, which looks like a tall, ragged hedge. Within this the Bulgarian keeps his domestic animals, — his oxen, cow, pig, and dog; and just by the hut may be seen a rude shed, where the grain is stowed away.

The huts, curiously enough, are mostly under ground; little except the roof is seen above the soil. Inside them, however, there is an air of cosiness and comfort; and what is better than all, of exceeding neatness.

The Bulgarians are of medium height, squarely built, with coarse features, and rather dark in complexion. The Tartars in the eastern part of the province are swarthy, with big black eyes and long hair and fierce-looking faces.

The usual dress of the men is a loose open jacket, of a dark color, a vest of like material, and trousers which are large and baggy as far as the knee, below which they fit tightly to the leg. A long sash is worn about the waist, and a round cap of sheepskin covers the head.

The women almost always appear in a shirt and bodice, a cloth tunic, and long skirt. They have a broad belt about the waist, and a gaudily colored apron in front. Their small red caps are often decorated with curious coins of various metals.

The Bulgarians are, it is true, ignorant, and show but little ambition; yet they have many excellent qualities. They are noted for their simple honesty, the steadiness with which they work, and for their temperance and morality. This is more than can be said of some nations that are much more highly civilized.

"I cannot understand," said Wyllys, "why the Turks have any power at all over these principalities. We meet at least three Christians everywhere to a single Turk."

"Turkey in Europe is but a small part of the Turkish Empire," said Master Lewis. "By the treaties that followed the last war, Servia, Montenegro, Bosnia, and Bulgaria are virtually made independent; and the Turkish power in Europe is reduced to a mere name."

"By visiting Novi Bazaar," said Wyllys, "we have had glimpses of all the principalities of which we have read much in the papers for the last few years, — and now we are passing through Roumelia."

"I planned the journey," said Master Lewis, "in this way, so that you might get a clear view of the history and politics of the East."

Salonica is the Thessalonica of the New Testament, a city in Macedonia, to which the Apostle Paul sent two epistles. It is the chief commercial emporium of the Turkish Empire. It is a funereal looking city; its walls, some five miles in extent, are shaded with cypresses, and over them rise mosques that were once Christian churches. Ruins are everywhere to be seen; and the appearance of the streets is miserable in the extreme. It has about seventy thousand inhabitants.

The Class here took the steamer for Constantinople, passing through the Dardanelles, that door to the East, that gate of dispute in each discussion of the Eastern Question.

The Dardanelles are the narrow straits which unite the Mediterranean Sea with the Sea of Marmora. The Sea of Marmora is connected, at its other end, with the Black Sea, by another narrow strait, called the Bosphorus; and it is upon this narrow strait of the Bosphorus that Constantinople, the Sultan's capital, is situated.

Thus the Dardanelles are an essential part of the water-way between the two great seas, — the Mediterranean and the Black Sea. The strait is about four miles wide at its broadest part, and a little less than a mile across at its narrowest point; and it is about forty miles long. It divides Europe from Asia, one of its shores being the famous peninsula of Gallipoli, and the other the furthest north-western coast of Asia Minor.

The Dardanelles were famous, in ancient times, as the Hellespont. It was across the principal strait, as most readers know, that Leander swam; and the same feat was afterwards performed, many centuries later, by the poet Lord Byron. When Xerxes invaded Europe, he built a bridge across the narrowest neck of the Hellespont. The name Dardanelles is supposed to have been given to the strait from the ancient province of Dardania, near by.

This narrow passage of water, situated as it is, has always been regarded as a military locality of great importance. Two of the earlier sultans, Mahomet II. and Mahomet IV., found it wise to defend its entrance at the Mediterranean end by erecting four formidable

A GARDEN OF BEAUTY.

forts, — two on the European and two on the Asiatic shore. These forts remain to this day; and although they might be unable to bar the intrusion of ironclads, they could stop merchant ships, transports, and all other vessels.

In modern times, the Dardanelles have served to greatly restrict the maritime movements of nations, and have been the subject of many treaties and more than one war.

It must be remembered that a large portion of the coast of the Black Sea, shut in as it is, and only accessible from the greater seas by the Dardanelles, belongs to Russia. The only other Russian seacoast is the Baltic, which is closed to navigation by ice the greater part of the year. The Black Sea, therefore, is the only place where Russia could maintain a powerful navy; nor can she do this, unless she is able to go in and out by the strait we have described.

For a long period, the sultans, supported by England (who has always opposed the creation of a Russian navy), kept the Dardanelles strictly closed to all foreign ships whatever. None could pass in or out of the strait. About fifty years ago there was a war between Russia and Turkey, the result of which was that Turkey was forced to agree that Russian *merchant* ships should be allowed to go in and out by the Dardanelles; but *war* ships were still excluded. Somewhat later it was agreed by all the Powers that the war ships of no nation should be allowed to enter the Dardanelles.

As a result of the defeat of Russia in the Crimea by France, England, and Turkey, twenty years ago, Russia was forbidden not only to send war ships in and out of the Dardanelles, but to have any war ships even in the Black Sea itself. This restriction was, however, removed in 1871; and since that year Russia has been able to have war ships in the Black Sea, but not to send them through the Dardanelles.

She now desires this privilege also; and should she obtain it, the result would be that Russia would build up a great navy, which would in time rival that of England herself. With the Black Sea as a vast dock-yard and arsenal, and a way to the Mediterranean and the Atlantic through the Dardanelles, she would, ere long, become one of the great naval powers of the earth.

We see in this the reason why the opening of the strait to Russian war vessels has been so long and is still opposed by England; and why the little strait has been a subject of such bitter contention for a long period of years.

So, leaving the Eastern Question again, we approach Constantinople.

The Class was in the land of stories. Turkey is as full of romances as of green woods and flowers. Most of these stories have been brought into the country from Asia; they have the wealth, glow, coloring of Persia, and more or less of the savor of the Golden Age of the Caliphs, and much of the airy charm of the "Arabian Nights."

We give here one of these Turkish romances, which much pleased the Class on its way to the Sea of Marmora and the Golden Horn.

NUMAN AND NAAM;

OR, THE OLD WOMAN WHO COULD TEACH TRICKS TO A FOX, AND THE WISE DOCTOR.

A very long time ago, in the times of the kings of the family of the Beni Ommieh, whatever family that might have been, there lived in the city of Cufah a young man named Numan, who had a most beautiful young wife. I say "most beautiful," for this is the simple English way of speaking of the woman; but such a phrase is as dust to gold, in comparison to the Oriental adjectives that describe her charms. We are told that

> "If ever there was a being *unique* in the world,
> A second like which sure never was seen,
> It was she, it was she."

This couple, we are also told, were like two "cedars in a garden of beauty;" and further, that her loveliness was so lustrous that her face shone in the dark,

MEDJADJ PASSING THE PALACE.

which I am a little afraid may not be quite true. Still, it was long, long ago, and it is pleasant to receive the old chronicler's testimony.

They lived in a palace, which we are informed was "like the gardens of Paradise." The lady's *name* was *Naam*, which you will be sure to remember; and it is related that, in addition to her personal beauty, she had a very melodious

NAAM'S PALACE.

voice, and when she sang by the palace window the people in the street stopped to listen; and, if they were not already married, they straightway fell in love. What a valuable lady she would be now, when so many bachelors are to be found!

The customs of the lands of the Mohammedan religion are not like ours. A rich man there may have many wives; and the caliph, who was the prince of the country, and was supposed to be the successor of Mohammed, the prophet, claimed the right to the handsomest women in his dominions for *his* wives. His officers of state were as ambitious to secure for him beautiful women to marry as to obtain the choicest gems for his sceptre and crown.

Now, the governor of the city of Cufah was Hedjadj, — pronounce it quickly, and so show your good school training. He was called "The Cruel." One day he was passing the palace where this happy couple lived, when he heard Naam singing.

He was quite enchanted.

"If that lady's face," said he, "is as beautiful as her voice, she is fit for the wife of the caliph."

Now, the Mohammedan women do not show their faces, except to their own household. They wear veils in the presence of strangers.

Hedjadj, therefore, instructed his chief of police to find a cunning woman, who would by some artifice secure a place in Naam's household, and report to him if the lady's face were as beautiful as her voice. If it were, he hoped to entice her away from her husband, and present her to the caliph.

There was an old woman in the city who was a sorceress. She was, we are told, "expert in all ways of deceit," and was so cunning that she could "teach tricks to a fox," which must have been very cunning indeed. She spent much of her time in the streets, and was very watchful for opportunities to enrich herself by her arts.

When the chief of police informed this old woman who was so cunning that she "could teach tricks to a fox" of the governor's wish, she answered, —

"If the object of your desires be in the skies among the Pleiades, under the earth, or on the earth, I will surely find her, and put her into your power," which was a very high-flying answer for the cunning old lady to make.

The old woman dressed herself to represent a *Sofy* — a sort of Mohammedan nun — an hundred years old. She put a shawl over her head, and took in her hand an iron-shod stick, and went into the street, exclaiming, —

"Listen, O ye people! Allah is one God! Listen, O ye people!"

In this disguise she came to Numan's palace, and asked to be admitted.

The servants refused her.

"Hear, O ye people! I have deserted the world. I am a servant of Allah. Wherever I bend my steps I carry good fortune; every one profits by my coming. Why do you obstruct my entrance?"

The servants admitted her, and conducted her to Naam.

Now, Naam was a truly good woman, with all of her beauty and accomplishments; and she delighted in the society of pious souls, hoping to profit by their experience.

The old woman gave her a salutation, and said, —

"Let not Allah be forgotten. Show me a retired place, where I may pray."

Naam spread a carpet for her in a closet; and the *Sofy* prayed in words and preyed in thought until noon, and from noon until night, which supposed devotion quite won the young wife's heart.

The old woman remained in the palace several days, — it seemed as if her devotions would never end. She then told Naam she must depart for a time.

"Where are you going?" asked Naam.

"To visit some pious people. Will you not go with me?"

NAAM'S GARDEN.

Naam gladly consented; her heart always responded to what promised hope and comfort to others.

The old woman led Naam to the house of the governor. When they reached the vestibule she said, —

"Remain here, and I will go and see if the good man is alone."

She found ready access to the "good" man, you may well believe. She told her story, and departed in secret. Hedjadj came to the vestibule, and, surprising Naam, saw her face, which we are told was so "resplendent" that it filled the "whole vestibule with splendor." We are also told that she appeared

"Fresh as a rose from the garden of truth,
And a thousand philomels were her lovers."

Hedjadj ordered his soldiers to seize poor Naam, and to get ready a litter, and carry her on it to Damascus, where was the palace of the caliph.

HOUSE OF THE GOVERNOR.

When Naam found how cruelly she had been deceived, she was struck to the heart with grief, and her tears flowed continually. The journey to Damascus was a long one, occupying thirty or forty days; and her mind continually dwelt on her husband, whom she dearly loved. The admiration which her beauty excited at the caliph's palace only increased her sorrow. The splendors of Damascus were nothing to her. The glories of the caliph's palace seemed a mockery in comparison with the light of love in her own happy home. She fell sick soon after her arrival, and her beauty began to wither.

The caliph was enchanted when he met her.

"Her teeth in brightness could make the stars envious,
Rose-buds opened when she smiled,
Jewels were scattered about when she spake."

So says the poet, and he ought to have been truthful; but we do not often see a lady quite so charming as that now.

We must now return to Numan. When he found that his lovely bride had been stolen, he shut himself up for grief, and youth faded from his cheek like the emerald tint from the autumn leaf. He must have a skilful physician, his friends said. Who should it be?

Now, however crafty may be the agents of evil, the spirit of good is mighty, and virtue is sure to triumph in the end. When those who have been deceived trust in Providence, there open to them golden doors and pleasant pathways out of all their troubles; and we are glad to say that Numan and Naam were very good people as Mohammedans go.

There came to Cufah at this time a very wise physician. The medicine venders in those days did not publish medical almanacs and advertise in the newspapers; but in a more direct, and quite as modest way, cried themselves in the streets. Now, this physician went about crying,—

"Let him appear who needs a skilful physician and one versed in the hidden sciences!"

The father of Numan heard this physician calling under the window, and he invited him to see his son. The physician declared that Numan had no disease of body, but was wasting of disappointment; and he declared that, if Allah would assist him, he must find the lost bride and restore her to her husband.

The wise and pious physician soon discovered the arts of the wicked old woman who could teach tricks to a fox, and learned whither Naam had been sent. He proposed to Numan that they should go in company to Damascus, and "see what the Lord would do for them."

Now the caliph had a very lovely sister named Abbassah. She pitied Naam, and tenderly nursed her. She sought for her the best medical aid; and now people began to hear of a great wonder that had come to Damascus. Two physicians had established themselves on a certain street, who healed all that applied to them for remedies. A slave brought the great news to the palace of the caliph. Abbassah heard it, and she resolved to send for one of these wonderful men to prescribe for Naam. The two doctors were the wise physician of Cufah and Numan.

HOUSE OF NUMAN'S FATHER.

When the servant of Abbassah summoned the physicians to the caliph's palace, the wise doctor went alone, and he found it was a young lady who needed the prescription, and, though he could not learn her name, he believed her to be Naam. When he went again, he carried a prescription in Numan's handwriting, which he ordered to be taken to the inner palace, where the lady dwelt. When the servant returned, she brought a purse of gold, and in the purse was found a secret note indicating, in a mystic way, that she understood the doctor's purpose. As soon as Naam saw the handwriting of the prescription, hope revived. The roses bloomed on her cheek again, and she caused it to be known in the inner palace, and to the caliph, that the new doctor's medicines were doing her much good.

Naam told her true history to her servant, who met the new doctors, for no man except the caliph was allowed to go into the inner palace. Numan also confided his history to the same servant, when he had learned that she had the heart and confidence of Naam. The two desired to meet; but this could not be, as no man was allowed to go into the inner palace, and no woman was permitted to pass out of it unattended. But Naam prayed continually that God, in his providence, would effect what seemed to be impossible.

One day the servant said to Naam, —

"Do you wish to see Numan?"

Naam replied, —

"Ask the sick if he wish for health."

The faithful servant answered, —

"No one should eat sorrow, for God will give aid. There is a remedy for every ill. I will weep until I see you smile."

When the servant met Numan, she said, —

"Do you wish to see Naam?"

"Yes; if it cost me my life."

"No one should eat sorrow, for God will give aid. There is a remedy for every ill. I will weep until I see you smile."

Then she said, —

"Come with me to the palace."

She threw a beautiful cloak over Numan, that gave him the appearance of a woman.

When they reached the gate of the inner palace, the porter asked who the new comer might be.

"One of the family of Naam, who has come to visit her," answered the servant.

The latter then directed Numan to Naam's apartments, and stood herself in the servants' hall to await his reappearance, and to conduct him out of the palace.

Numan did not well understand the direction. He passed by the apartments of Naam and entered the room of Abbassah, the caliph's sister. The apartment was hung with brocade and silk, and furnished with luxurious sofas, and glittered with golden ornaments. Presently Abbassah entered.

"What foolish woman are you, that without permission have entered my room?"

"I am no woman, but a wretched man, in great trouble and sorrow. I came here because my heart is grieved, and my spirit groans. My bride has been stolen from me, and I have traced her here; and I have thus risked my life to once more behold her. Blame me not. In my case you would feel as I feel, and do as I have done."

Numan then told her his story, and the lady's eyes filled with tears.

"Do not fear," she said; "you have a true heart, and I will protect you. I will send at once for Naam."

The meeting of the happy pair is described in glowing language in the original romance, too flowery in fact for practical people nowadays to appreciate. We are told that when they saw each other each fell senseless to the floor, and that Abbassah threw rose-water in their faces, which was a very proper thing to do; and that both recovered, which was also very proper. Naam took her lute and began to sing.

As she was singing, a majestic step approached the door, and a loud voice called, —

"Barik Allah" (whatever that may mean)! "What voices are those I hear?"

Abbassah was startled by the voice. She knew it was the caliph. She threw a cloak around Numan, and advanced to meet her brother.

"Go on with your pastimes," said the caliph.

"O Emir of the Faithful!" said Abbassah. "I am about to tell a story. Listen! for I want your judgment upon the points that I shall present.

"O Emir of the Faithful! there once lived a young man in Cufah who had a lovely bride. One night the governor of the city, a wicked and cruel man, was making his rounds, when he chanced to pass near the window of the palace where the happy pair lived, and to hear the lady singing. The next day he employed an old woman, who was reputed to be so artful that she could teach tricks to a fox, to entice this young bride from the palace, which she did by pretending an errand of charity; and when he found her in his power he sent her as a present to the caliph."

"Had I been the caliph, I would have restored her to her home," said the emir.

"Yes, Emir of the Faithful, you would have done justly. But listen! A wise doctor, who believed that the powers of good were mightier than those of evil, learned whither the bride had been carried. He induced the sorrowing husband to go with him to the city, where the caliph held his court, and try to recover his young wife. When they had arrived, they were led to believe that it would be death to approach the caliph in such a cause."

"I would have received the husband graciously."

"Yes, Emir of the Faithful, you would have been gracious. But listen! This man from Cufah, in the disguise of a woman, came into the palace at the peril of his life to see his bride. He succeeded in meeting her; but during the interview the caliph himself appeared, and the ruse was discovered."

Abbassah paused.

"And what did the caliph do?"

"He drew his sword and slew them."

"What an ignorant ruler! The two persons were excusable. He should have learned their story, and have done them justice."

"Emir of the Faithful, that is what you would have done?"

"Yes; a caliph should be merciful and just."

"Then behold such a case before you!"

Abbassah drew aside the cloak from Numan, and revealed to the astonished eyes of the caliph,—a man.

"Behold!" she said, "in the youth before you the subject of my story, and in this woman the stolen bride. O Prince of the Faithful! by your own promise may your justice never pass by the innocent. The governor of Cufah has treated these as I have told you; what shall be done, not to these unfortunate people, but to Hedjadj ez Zalim?"

"He shall be driven from his office; and the wise physician shall have his place."

"Allah is just! And what shall be done with Numan and Naam?"

"They shall be restored to their palace; and the God who heareth the cry of the just shall be praised."

CONSTANTINOPLE

CHAPTER IX.

CONSTANTINOPLE.

CONSTANTINOPLE. — THE DERVISHES. — TOMMY'S LETTER.

HE situation of Constantinople is the most beautiful in all the world.

Look upon the map of Turkey, and you will find Kadi Keny. It was once called Chalcedon. It is on the Sea of Marmora, nearly opposite Constantinople, and is inferior to that city in situation, though it was founded before it.

Nearly seven hundred years before Christ, an oracle is said to have told some Megarian emigrants a very strange thing.

"Found your city," it said, "opposite the land of the blind men."

They went in search of the "land of the blind men." They came to Chalcedon, and saw beyond it the beautiful situation for a city in the curve of the Golden Horn. Then they understood the meaning of the oracle; and they founded Byzantium, opposite Chalcedon. The city grew, and nearly a thousand years afterwards became the capital of the Byzantine Empire, as Greece and the Roman provinces in the East were called. This empire was founded in 395, when Theodosius the Great divided the Roman Empire between his two sons, Arcadius and Honorius, giving the former the East and the latter the West.

As the traveller approaches Constantinople, he first sees the slender minarets, or tall spires, from which the Mohammedans are called to prayer, glimmering like jewelled fingers in the sun. Then he beholds the swelling domes of the mosques. Mosque and minaret are surmounted by crescents: the air glowing over the Golden Horn is, as it were, full of moons.

Why is this emblem everywhere seen?

In the year 340 B. C. the Macedonians laid siege to the city. They prepared to carry the walls by assault one cloudy night, and take the place by surprise. Just as the attack was about to be made, the clouds parted, and the crescent moon shone clear on the city, revealing the plan of the enemy. The people believed that the appearance of the crescent at this time was a revelation of Divine favor. They made the crescent their emblem, and placed it in their temples, and engraved it on their shields. When the Turks captured the city, and overthrew the Byzantine or Eastern Empire, they, too, adopted the crescent as their emblem, and set it on every minaret as a symbol of the favor of God.

The streets of Byzantium, or Constantinople, have been purpled by wars for twenty-five hundred years. It would take a long history to present a view of these contests. The city was besieged by the Roman emperors Severus, Maximus, and Constantinus; by the Persians, Avars, and Arabs. It fell under the power of Rome with the whole of the Grecian Empire; and Constantine in 330 made it the capital of the Roman Empire, and so of the world. It was attacked again and again by Russia, and was conquered by the Latin Crusaders. It was recovered by the Greeks in 1261; and in the spring of 1453 it fell before the conquering sword of Mahomet II. It was once the head of the Latin Church; it has been for many centuries the principal seat of the Mohammedan power.

St. Sophia! The House of Wisdom, it was called, for *Sophia* means wisdom. A hundred miles distant on the sea, the sailor may see the crescent on the principal cupola glimmering in the sun. The gold on this crescent alone cost a fortune; and other fortunes glitter in the crescents below.

GOLDEN HORN, FROM A KIOSQUE IN THE SERAGLIO.

The Church of St. Sophia was the pride of the East, when the Byzantine Empire divided the world with Rome. It was believed to have been built under the direction of angels. Its foundations were laid during the reign of Constantine, or about the year 325, the year of the Council of Nice. It was twice burned, but only to arise in greater splendor, until the present edifice began to grow, and drew to it the spoils of many temples and climes. All the beautiful marbles of the East were sought for: Phrygian white marble, with rose-colored seams; black Celtic marble, with white veins; Bosphorus marble, with black veins; Egyptian starred granite and Saitic porphyry. Columns from the Temple of the Sun at Baalbec; from the Temple of Diana at Ephesus; from the temples at Athens, and thus from the temples of the Sun and Moon, and of Isis and Osiris and Olympian Jove. A hundred architects superintended it, under whom were placed a hundred masons. An angel, the emperor claimed, came to him and revealed the plan in a dream or vision. The angel appeared again, and this time, if we may follow the tradition, revealed a subterranean vault full of gold, eighty hundredweight in quantity, which was used to complete the dome. The cupolas were things of air. The tiles were of extraordinary lightness. The main cupola, indeed, seems to be suspended in the air. It is a marvel of human skill.

The altar was withdrawn from the eyes of the people by a partition, in which were twelve gold columns. The sacred vessels were of gold; and the chalice cloths, of which there were forty-two thousand, were worked in jewels. There were doors of ivory, amber, and cedar, and doors veneered with planks which were said to have been taken from Noah's ark. Justinian originally intended to pave the floor with plates of gold, but used instead waving lines of marble, representing the advance of the sea. It was lighted with candelabra of gold.

"God be praised!" said the emperor, on the day of its dedication. "Solomon, I have surpassed thee!"

It was dedicated on Christmas. A thousand oxen, a thousand

sheep, and ten thousand birds were killed, and thirty thousand measures of corn, and three hundred hundredweight of gold were divided among the people.

But God dwells not in temples made by hands, but in the heart. The Eastern Church lost her spirituality, and forsook virtue, and this new Solomon's temple became the spoil of the Mohammedan, who made it a mosque. To-day it is a show, a monument of the old Byzantine age of art and worldly glory, and of the departed opulence of the sultans.

The Class descended some steps on entering the edifice, and then went to the *gynaikites*, as the female gallery was called, in the middle of which the magnificence of the edifice appeared.

"If I do not believe that the building was planned by angels," said Wyllys. "I could almost be persuaded to think that angels held the dome in the air. Look, — it rests on nothing."

And so it seemed.

"No Christian church, not even St. Peter's," said Master Lewis, "ever equalled this in beauty in the days of the emperors; and I doubt if any other structure of the kind ever will. The age of temples is gone. The world is learning that the temple of God is the soul; and that the truth that Christ told the woman of Samaria is the only principle of acceptable worship."

The ancient palace of the sultans, or seraglio, whose enclosure is three miles in circumference, — which is washed on one side by the Sea of Marmora and on the other by the Golden Horn, and whose airy courts are gardens of velvety palms, vine-covered cypresses, and all varieties of odorous roses, — next drew the Class from the hotel. It was like a city of pavilions, and seemed fashioned as from a dream. The golden crescent glimmered over all these courts of color and aerial splendor, carvings, arabesques, balconies, and fountains.

Tommy wrote the members of the Class, who were travelling in Germany or Switzerland, a letter, giving somewhat in detail the story of his adventures in the Sultan's city. We will give it here: —

PARLOR IN THE SERAGLIO

CONSTANTINOPLE, July —, 18—.

To the Boys of the Class:

I have been in Constantinople four days, and I, 1st, have been lost; 2d, have taken a Turkish bath; 3d, have heard the dervishes howl.

It is very hot here just now; but Constantinople is a very interesting city, indeed, to the traveller, especially to the *young* traveller.

1. *How I got lost.* As soon as we arrived, Master Lewis was surrounded by a crowd of men with shining eyes and clothes like rag-bags. Some officers opened his portmanteaus, and the crowd presently beset him, their arms swinging like wind-mills, and their tongues going like clappers. Each one wished to be hired as a guide; and each said the other was a pretty dangerous fellow, — had been in prison, committed murder, or done some villanous thing; and I should think from their looks that they all spoke the truth.

Well, amid all this racket and the long delay, I thought I would take my first glimpse of the streets of the city. I had heard of the Golden Horn, and I rather fancied that the streets might be something like gold in appearance, for the city at a distance looked like a pile of gold and marble.

There did not seem to be any streets. It was something like Marblehead, where the houses are set down in the middle of the road, and every house stands in a square or a square path of rock that goes around it.

I thought I would just walk around a few of these queer houses, and after I had done so I did not know where I was. The lanes were full of dogs, that looked as though they wanted something to eat; and I trod on one dog's tail, and he howled and opened his long mouth, and I was afraid he was about to eat me. I walked around house after house, hoping to find the place where I had left Master Lewis; but each lane was a little queerer and stranger than the other, and I began to be confused, and knew not what to do.

I now began to say to each person I met, "*Hotel de Luxembourg.*"

I spoke the words in English and in French. But the men in big pantaloons just stared and chattered, and I could make nothing of their gibberish, any more than as though they had been the barbarians that they looked to be.

At last I saw a group of men, and among them was one that looked like a sailor. I hurried to him.

"Will you tell me how to find the French hotel?" said I. "I am lost."

"The Luxembourg?" he asked, in English.

"Yes; I will pay you for your trouble."

"I never take pay for helping a man in trouble," said he; and he led me through the queerest ways I ever saw, and left me at the Luxembourg.

There are some clever people in the world. That man never expected to see me again; *that* is what I call natural goodness of heart.

I explained my situation at the hotel, and asked that a *commissionnaire* be sent to Master Lewis to *tell him I had arrived*.

When he arrived he did not look nearly as agreeable as the sailor, but he only said, "Tommy, how could you do so!"

In the evening Master Lewis and Wyllys took a Turkish bath. The next morning they told me what a delightful thing it was, and how it reacted and brought refreshing sleep.

Wyllys said, "It makes you feel as though you were *created anew*."

So, in the morning, as I had not slept well and did not feel well, I thought I would like to be created anew, and I was taken in charge of a servant to undergo the wonderful bath.

I was led into a very pleasant apartment, where I left my clothes, and then was conducted slowly through a long passage-way that began to grow very hot; and I felt as I did once when I was going to have the fever.

Then an evil-eyed man took me and laid me on a kind of table that looked very cool, but that was just about as hot as the top of a cooking-stove; or so it seemed to me. I had no sooner touched it than I bounded off again.

"The thing is hot, — hot as blazes," said I.

I began to examine myself to see if I was *scorched*, when the evil-eyed man poured some water on the apparatus, and caught me up and put me on it again. Another dark-eyed man came to his assistance, and they covered me all over with soap; and then they began to pound me. How would you like to have been put on the top of a range, and pounded all over by two of the most crazy-looking men you ever saw?

But this was not all. They began to *crack* my joints; I could hear my bones *crack*. I wondered if I were to be all broken up before being "created anew."

Then I was bathed, which was very refreshing; and I began to feel rich, easy, and happy, as though this was a rather pleasant world after all, and that life was just the thing to have if you could have enough of it. I was all aglow.

There was a queer-looking barber's shop at the end of the apartments, and I thought I would just look in and see how people were shaved in the East. What do you think I saw? The black-visaged barber was shaving the top of a man's head off. I mean the hair on the top of the man's head. He left one little tuft. I asked Master Lewis afterward what the tuft was left for, and he said it was for the "angel of the resurrection."

While I was looking at the barbarous process, one of the men who had roasted me, soaped me, and cracked my joints, took me by the hand and led me through the door of the barber's room, pointing to an empty chair.

Master Lewis did not have his head shaved. Nor Wyllys. *I* would not. I hung back, and shook my head at the barbarian. I gave a sudden jerk, and twisted my hand out of his, and run. Did n't I run!

In the apartment where I had left my clothes, I found the French servant. I shall not visit the place again. Still, I did feel good all the rest of the day, and I do not remember anything about the night. I think I rested well.

DERVISHES

Yesterday was Friday, the Turkish Sabbath. We went to Pera, as the diplomatic quarter of the city is called. The palaces of the foreign ambassadors are there, — English, French, Russian, etc. In the High Street of Pera is a *tekeh*, or convent of dervishes.

The dervishes are an order of monks, who work themselves up into a nervous frenzy, and then spin round like a top. There were some twenty of them.

On the previous day we saw the howling dervishes at Skutari, as one of the suburbs is called.

They entered the chapel slowly, led by their high priest. They then fell upon the floor, while the priest repeated a long prayer. Then they began to wail, and rock their bodies to and fro. Their eyes seemed to gleam, and, will you believe it, they actually foamed at the mouth!

They seemed to be crying "*Al'lah-hou!*" They shouted this word louder and louder, and faster and faster, until their voices seemed to fail, and to blend in one low howl.

Then the sound rose again, something like this, — "*Lah-il lah il l Al'lah!*" It seemed like nothing earthly. Presently, one of them gave a shriek, and fell right over in a dreadful fit; then another, and another. Was n't that a sight for a doctor! Master Lewis said that one of their exercises, which they sometimes performed, was to repeat the ninety-nine names of Allah ninety-nine times. I would not like to go to a dervish Sunday school. Constantinople does not look like a place that has many Sunday schools. I think it would pay to send a few missionaries there.

But there is one good thing about the people. They let all the dogs live, which is very humane; and the consequence is that there is a lot of them (I mean dogs).

We visited Skutari not only to see the dervishes, but also to be able to say we had been in Asia. We saw there a Turkish cemetery, full of cypresses and beautiful white marble tomb-stones. These stones look very odd at a little distance; they seem larger at the top than at the base; and some of the old ones look as if they were *reeling*.

Did you ever see the puzzle called the Horizontorium? It is like a Turkish tomb-stone. I send you one, — the puzzle, not the tomb-stone.

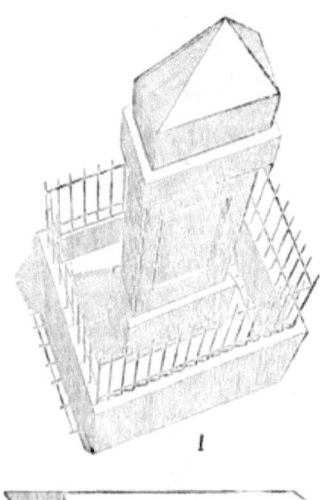
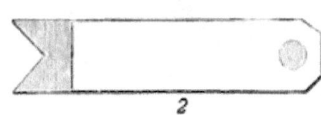

HORIZONTORIUM.

Now you can make this ill-proportioned figure present the appearance of a neat, well-shaped tomb-stone, enclosed by an upright fence. To do this, a sight-piece should first be prepared. It can be cut from thick paper, the shape of the diagram in the illustration numbered 2. The end of this sight-piece should be bent so that it will stand upright, and then it can be held by gluten to the spot marked 3 in the picture.

Let the paper rest upon the table, close one eye, and look steadily with the other at the tomb-stone through the little hole at the top of the sight-piece. A well-proportioned tomb-stone, surrounded by an upright railing, will be seen. The tomb-stone will not only appear well-proportioned, but will seem to *stand out* from the paper, as though viewed by a stereoscope.

The mosques are gorgeous. St. Sophia is like Aladdin's palace. The seraglio, or Sultan's palace, is large enough for a town; a whole city of art, nearly three miles in circuit. But one dislikes to see all of this splendor in a city of poor people, half fed and half clothed.

The entrance to the seraglio, or the palace gate, is called the *Porte*, — the *Sublime Porte*. The Turkish Sultan does not administer justice at this gate; but the government is, nevertheless, called the Porte.

Master Lewis speaks of you all, often. If ever a teacher loved his work and his pupils, it is he. He read to Wyllys and me a poem from a note-book as we were sailing down the Danube, which relates his experience as a scholar and a teacher. He allowed me to copy it; and, as you may learn from it how fine a regard he has for us all, I will close my letter with it. It will carry you back to Massachusetts, and cause you to agree with me when I say that, with all the palaces, monuments, cathedrals, mosques, and splendors of Europe, there is nothing quite so good as a New-England school.

With affectionate regards,
TOMMY.

THE BEAUTIFUL VILLAGE OF YULE.

My springtime of life has departed, —
  Its romance has ended at last;
My dreamings were once of the future,
  But now they are all of the past;
And memory oft in my trials
  Goes back to my pastimes at school,
And pictures the children who loved me
  In the beautiful village of Yule.

The schoolhouse still stands by the meadow,
    And green is the spot where I played,
And flecked with the sun is the shadow
    Of the evergreen woods where I strayed.
The thrush in the meadowy places
    Still sings in the evergreens cool,
But changed are the fun-loving faces
    Of the children who met me at Yule.

I remember the day, when, a teacher,
    I met those dear faces anew;
The warm-hearted greetings that told me
    The friendships of childhood are true.
I remember the winters I struggled,
    When careworn and sick, in my school:
I remember the children who loved me
    In the beautiful village of Yule.

So true, in the days of my sadness,
    Did the hearts of my trusted ones prove.
My sorrow grew light in the gladness
    Of having so many to love.
I gave my own heart to my scholars,
    And banished severity's rule,
And happiness dwelt in my schoolroom,
    In the beautiful village of Yule.

I taught them the goodness of loving
    The beauty of nature and art;
They taught me the goodness of loving
    The beauty that lies in the heart:
And I prize more than lessons of knowledge
    The lessons I learned in my school, —
The warm hearts that met me at morning,
    And left me at evening, in Yule.

I remember the hour that we parted:
    I told them, while moistened my eye,
That the bell of the schoolroom of glory
    Would ring for us each in the sky.
Their faces were turned to the sunset,
    As they stood 'neath the evergreens cool:
I shall see them no more as I saw them,
    In the beautiful village of Yule.

FOUNTAIN IN THE SERAGLIO.

The bells of the schoolroom of glory
  Their summons have rung in the sky.
The moss and the fern of the valley
  On some of the old pupils lie:
Some have gone from the wearisome studies
  Of earth to the happier school;
Some faces are bright with the angels',
  Who stood in the sunset at Yule.

I love the instructions of knowledge,
  The teachings of nature and art,
But more than all others the lessons
  That come from an innocent heart.
And still to be patient and loving
  And trustful I hold as a rule,
For so I was taught by the children
  Of the beautiful village of Yule.

My spring-time of life has departed, —
  Its romance has ended at last:
My dreamings were once of the future,
  But now they are all of the past.
Methinks when I stand in life's sunset,
  As I stood when we parted at school,
I shall see the bright faces of scholars
  I loved in the village of Yule.

CHAPTER X.

THE BLACK SEA.

TOMMY TALKS POLITICS. — ODESSA. — THE BLACK SEA AND THE CITY OF GRAVES.

NE summer morning, while the light mist hung over the Golden Horn, the Class sailed away on the Odessa steamer. The city of the Sultan, so soon to fall, like ripe fruit, into Christian hands; the golden crescents, so soon to be changed again to star-like crosses; the shore of Asia, certain to become the scene of new conflicts, — faded away, and the immense distances of the Black Sea opened from the gate of the Bosphorus.

Master Lewis had chosen to visit Sebastopol by the way of Odessa, as he considered the travelling accommodation safer and better by this route. At Odessa he would take one of the fine steamers of the Russian Steam Navigation Company for the Crimea.

The Black Sea, or Euxine, — the *Pontus Euxinus* of the ancients, and the Hospitable Sea of all times, — is in shape like the human foot, is seven hundred miles long, and has but a single island. It is a lovely sheet of water in summer, bright and calm, almost without winds, and wholly without tides. In the winter it is the scene of conflicting winds, and its shores are glittering ice walls.

As the scenes on the Bosphorus disappeared, Wyllys and Tommy began to ask many questions concerning the political history of the country to which they were going.

"I do not exactly know why," said Tommy, "but in all I have learned about the Eastern Question, my sympathies go with Russia. I like Russia."

"I feel like Tommy in this respect," said Wyllys. "I like Russia. She freed the serfs, secured to the Christian provinces of Turkey their rights, and was friendly to the United States in the War for the Union. I should think any one would not long hesitate in a question of sympathy between the Russian and the Turk. Just study the face of one and then of the other. It always makes me indignant to hear of the support that England has given to Mohammedanism in Europe."

"At first sight," said Master Lewis, "it seems strange that two countries so far apart as England and Russia, with traits and aims so differ-

NATIONAL EMBLEM OF RUSSIA

ent, should find themselves in each other's way. But a little reflection will show good reasons for their mutual hostility.

"The main reason why they dread and fear each other lies in the fact that England has obtained, and is resolved to keep, possession of India, and that she suspects Russia of coveting that splendid province.

"For many years Russia has been making conquests in Central Asia, the southern borders of which touch the frontiers of India. Gradually but steadily the Russian armies have approached the great chain of mountains which separate India from Turkestan, subjecting the various tribes, as they were reached, and placing Russian governors and garrisons over them.

"This danger to the English rule in India, however, has been but a vague and remote one until within recent years.

"Russia has shown an ambition in another direction, which has not less alarmed the English, and which was the cause of the Crimean War.

"I told you that Peter the Great, the able and warlike monarch who founded the Russian Empire, left it as a mission to his successors, to conquer Constantinople, and to make that ancient city the capital of the Greek Church. No attempt was made, however, to do this until the haughty Emperor Nicholas came to the throne.

"England has deemed it her policy to sustain Turkey against any attack by Russia; and that is why England is so anxious when the Christian subjects of Turkey are engaged in rebellion. She fears lest Russia may take advantage of the rebellion to interfere, destroy the Sultan's power, and at last capture and hold Constantinople.

"Several things have happened recently to increase the bitter feeling between the two countries.

"The marriage of the Czar's only daughter, and favorite child, with the Duke of Edinburgh, Queen Victoria's second son, has not proved altogether a happy one; and far from cementing a friendship between the two families, as was hoped, it resulted in a renewed coolness, not only between the royal families, but between the nations.

"The assumption by Queen Victoria of the title of Empress of India, also, is looked upon in Russia as a threat; and Mr. Disraeli's assertion that the object of this is to outbid Russia in the respect of the Hindoos gave rise to much indignation in that country.

GREAT SEAL OF ANCIENT RUSSIA.

"It seems probable that sooner or later England and Russia will come into collision, either in Turkey or in Asia. Events seem to be drawing towards a war between them, in which, perhaps, the fate not only of the Sultan's empire, but that of England in India, will be involved."

"What were the causes that led to the Crimean War?" asked Wyllys.

"I am glad you asked the question," said Master Lewis, "as in a few days we hope to visit the Crimea.

"However kindly we may feel towards Russia, we will have to acknowledge that Nicholas I., the father of the present noble Emperor, was proud, ambitious, and tyrannical. He crushed the heroic efforts of the Polish nation to gain its independence. By a ukase, in 1832, he declared the kingdom of Poland a Russian province, without diet or army. In 1849 he sent an army to aid Austria in her war against the Hungarians. Now, the sympathies of most people with democratic feelings, in these wars, were with the Poles and Hungarians.

"In 1853 Russia demanded of the Turkish government that it should protect the Greek Church in Turkey, and that it should guarantee this protection by a compact with the Czar."

"That seems to me a very right proceeding," said Tommy. "I have been reading about the merciless slaughters of the Christians in Turkey by the Turks."

"The demands of Russia were such as to affect the independence of Turkey as a nation, and to make the Czar, instead of the Sultan, the protector of the Christians in Turkey. Of course, the Porte refused to surrender its power over its subjects. Russia declared war. France, England, and Sardinia sided with Turkey."

"Christian nations took the part of Mohammedanism?" asked Tommy.

"Yes. The Turks are men, and Turkey is a nation. It had been agreed in the diplomacy of Europe, that the integrity of the Turkish

Empire, or its existence as an independent nation, should be maintained. Russia, in declaring war, seemed about to violate this understanding, and to destroy that balance of power that the European nations had agreed to sustain. This was culminated in the siege and capture of Sebastopol."

"I think Russia was right," said Tommy.

"And so do I," said Wyllys. "The Christians in Turkey were the slaves to the bloody and superstitious Mohammedans."

"What would you have thought of the conduct of England, if, thirty years ago, she had demanded that America should make a treaty with her to free the slaves in the South, and, in case of refusal, had declared war? Would you not have wished to maintain the independence of the nation?"

"I don't know," said Tommy; "but my feelings go with Russia."

"So I perceive; but where there are many nations on the same soil, without any natural boundaries, the integrity and independence of the weaker must be maintained by the stronger; and no one nation, on whatever pretext, must be allowed to put in peril the peace of the others. A Mohammedan has national rights."

"What you say," said Tommy, "goes to my head, but it does not go to my heart."

Master Lewis smiled.

"You called Nicholas a tyrant," said Tommy. "You wished me to read Wallace's 'Russia.' I have, in part.

"This is the manner Wallace speaks of Nicholas," continued Tommy, producing the book: "'In European politics he saw two forces struggling for mastery, monarchy, and democracy, which were, in his opinion, identical with order and anarchy; and he was always ready to assist his brother sovereigns in putting down democratic movements. In his own empire he endeavored, by every means in his power, to prevent the introduction of the dangerous ideas. For this purpose a stringent intellectual quarantine was established on the

THE WINTER PALACE.

western frontier. All foreign books and newspapers, except those of the most harmless kind, were rigorously excluded.'"

"'Assist his brother sovereigns in putting down democratic movements!'" exclaimed Master Lewis, with a curl of the lip. "'A stringent intellectual quarantine was established!' — lovely statements these for republican ears. If you had been one of the Poles or Hungarians, you would have known what 'assisting his brother sovereigns' meant, to your sorrow; as for 'intellectual quarantines,' suppose I were to try one on you?"

Tommy smiled.

"There was one good thing can be said about Nicholas; he respected the same boldness in others of which he was conscious in himself."

Odessa is the principal commercial city in the south of Russia, having a population of about 121,000. It is a fine-looking city from the sea; but in all their journeys the Class never passed so disagreeable a night as here. The heat was intense, — over one hundred degrees; the streets were full of dust, and each cooling breeze brought such a cloud of dust as to afford but little relief.

At eight A. M. on the day after their arrival, the Class took a very inviting-looking steamer for Sebastopol. The boat had a gentlemen's and a ladies' cabin, each handsomely furnished, ample decks, with a piano in the connecting saloon. The passengers were mostly Russians; and although the boys could not understand their language, they spoke of them as though they were somehow "long-lost brothers," or, rather, national friends. There was a nice library on board, which afforded the boys about as much information as the passengers.

Sebastopol is about 190 miles south-east of Odessa, and has a population of less than ten thousand. The dead soldiers in the cemeteries greatly outnumber the inhabitants of the historic city. Sebastopol is a place of graves. The Class found here a good hotel. One of the gentlemen here was a German, who spoke English. He was a

Russian in Eastern politics; and Tommy was happy in making his early acquaintance.

He, like all Germans, had a great admiration for the Czar and aversion to the Czarowitz.

"Alexander and *your* President Lincoln will live in history as the noblest men of this century."

Tommy's face glowed.

"Tell me all about Alexander," he said. "I do not know much about his history; I only know I admire him."

"And cannot exactly tell the reason why," said Master Lewis, in an undertone.

"He is the best of all the Romanoffs," said the gentleman. "He had the plan of emancipation in his heart when he was only nine years of age."

STORIES OF ALEXANDER.

Sitting, one morning, at breakfast with the Emperor and Empress, he was observed to be thinking instead of eating.

"What are your thoughts, my son?" asked his mother.

After some hesitation he replied that he was thinking how, when he became emperor, he would free all his poor countrymen who were slaves.

His parents were startled by his answer, and earnestly questioned him whence he obtained this idea. He assured them that he had learned it in church and from the Word of God, which teaches us to love our neighbors as ourselves.

The subject was not again alluded to; but no sooner had Alexander succeeded to the throne than he sent for a man of well-known piety and talent, and with his aid devised the vast scheme which has been a source of happiness to many millions.

It is a proof how greatly this measure has conduced to the prosperity of the country, that since it was effected, over eleven thousand miles of railroad have been built, and eight thousand miles more are in process of construction.

Better still, the liberated serfs have already established over fifteen thousand schools for the children, and the number is still increasing.

VIEW OF PLEVNA.

The Emperor's noble nature seems to be inherited by at least one of his sons. Some time ago the ship on which his third son, Alexis, was serving as midshipman, was wrecked on the coast of Denmark. The admiral had the lifeboats lowered, and ordered Alexis to take charge of the first. But this the midshipman refused to do, saying that it would not become the son of the Emperor to be the first to leave the ship; he should remain till the last. Notwithstanding the admiral's threat to put him in arrest for disobedience, he persisted in his determination; and on their reaching the shore the rigid discipline was enforced. The Emperor was informed as soon as possible of the facts, and telegraphed in reply,—

"I approve the act of the admiral in placing the midshipman under arrest for disobedience of orders, and I bless and kiss my son for disobeying them."

The night before he freed the serfs, not knowing but the ukase might lead to his assassination, he went into the chapel and remained there for a long time in prayer.

But with all of good will for his people I do not doubt that he is one of the most unhappy men in the empire. He can hardly have seen a peaceful year since he was made happy and hopeful for the future over the victory at Plevna. That Turkish battle-field must be the last green spot in the memory of the past; for years his constant care has been to elude his enemies.

His days are spent in the most harrowing suspense; and his nights must often be sleepless, and haunted by hideous fears. Three times, within ten months, his life was deliberately aimed at by assassins; seven times, during his reign, he has nearly become a victim either of the bullet, the dagger, or the mine.

He knows that everywhere about him lurk men and women, not in the lower ranks alone, but people of rank and wealth, who hope for an opportunity to deal him a death-blow. Death, indeed, may be at any time hidden in the dishes of which he partakes, in the wine or water he drinks, in the very envelopes he opens; under the floor beneath his feet, behind his bed-curtains, in the secrecy of his private cabinet, as well as on the public street, as he whirls rapidly by in his carriage.

A year ago it was the Czar's custom freely to walk the streets in the neighborhood of his palace, often unattended; as recently as that, he could still rely upon the veneration and love of his subjects.

He is never now seen thus trusting himself in public. Much of the time he keeps himself gloomily secluded in his palace, guarded by grim soldiery on every side; and even then a constant prey to a thousand shadowy fears. He never emerges into the street unless attended by a heavy escort of Cossacks, and preceded, followed, surrounded by open and secret police.

His food and drink are always tasted by some attendant before he ventures to partake of them. The closest watch is kept on every way of access to him. Since the very dining-room of his palace was blown up by an explosion, from which he and his family had the narrowest possible escape,—and the perpetrators of which have not been and cannot be discovered,—no precaution has been considered too minute to protect him from assassination.

It is well known that this constant and unseen peril to his life makes the Czar wretched, almost to insanity. More than once he has resolved to abdicate, but has been dissuaded from doing so by his advisers and by his own pride, which survives amid all his misery. He would surely be far happier if he should leave the cares as well as the glories of so thorny a crown, and retire to the rest and security of private life; but then his son, who would succeed him, would also inherit the dangers and murderous attempts to which he himself is now subject.

That so good a man, and so gentle a sovereign, as the Czar Alexander should thus be in constant jeopardy, makes it certain that it is the system which he represents, and not he himself, that is aimed at by the Nihilist conspirators.

He suffers for the cruelties and oppressions of a long line of ruthless and despotic ancestors.

"I grow more and more interested in Russia," said Tommy to Master Lewis, after his conversation with the affable German. "I have two other questions to ask,—

"What is Nihilism?

"Who are the Nihilists?"

"You are getting deep into Eastern politics, indeed," said Master Lewis. "Nihilism is the evidence of a spirit of unrest, dissatisfaction, and revolution among the Russians, who see all nations around them free, while they themselves are still kept in the bondage of a dreary absolutism.

"The revolt thus so mysteriously and bloodily begun will probably go on till the Russians, too, gain their liberty; and until this is at-

TREBIZOND SEASHORE.

tained, probably every czar must lead a life of constant danger and harrowing dread.

"What the Socialists are in Germany, the 'Nihilists' are in Russia. A 'Nihilist' is one who is supposed to believe in nothing; and the Russian Nihilist is one who is eager to overturn all the political and social institutions which he finds now existing. Many Nihilists do not believe in God, or in marriage, property, moral law, or government. They wish to overturn and change everything. Others who do not hold these views in regard to religion and society are Nihilists, because the order represents republican principles.

"He professes atheism for the same reason that the secret societies of the French Revolution professed it,— because he thinks the Church an instrument of rulers for the purposes of despotism. He, of course, can hardly believe it in his heart."

"One would not think," said Wyllys, "that such a society could be very numerous."

"But it is true," said Master Lewis, "that, in the great empire of Russia, which is supposed to be ruled by the Czar with an iron hand, there are thousands, probably even millions, of Nihilists.

"They comprise, indeed, a most extensive and powerful organization. There is scarcely a town or village throughout the empire where there is not a Nihilistic club or committee.

"There is a perfect net-work of Nihilistic committees all over the country, which is divided up into sections, ruled over by a higher committee. At St. Petersburg is a committee which overlooks and commands all the rest. It issues its decrees to the others; and whatever it commands is at once obeyed. These committees all act with the greatest secrecy; and the members of it are not even known to the body of Nihilists whom it commands.

"All the movements and objects of this terrible society, indeed, are hidden in the greatest mystery, and defy the keenest search of the Imperial police. Suddenly, the committee of a certain district will receive from the central body at St. Petersburg an order to stir up an insurrection, and will be provided by it with arms and ammunition for the purpose. It acts upon the order at once, and the revolt takes place.

"A Nihilist is commanded to kill some government official, or other person obnoxious to the league. He does not know, and does not ask, why this dark deed is to be done. He simply takes his pistol or his dagger, goes off quietly, and kills the designated victim.

"It would be a mistake to suppose that the Nihilists are confined entirely or commonly to one social class, or to the male sex. No doubt the great body of the society is composed of laborers and peasants. But it also includes a very large number of educated men, many men of property, and some men of high rank. There are within its secret circle learned professors, university students, lawyers, doctors, scholars, and philosophers. Princes and nobles have been detected in communion with the Nihilists, who can count among them some government officials, who receive salaries from the Czar.

"There are not only men, but many women, in the ranks of Nihilism. Ladies of high social position, and intelligent and delicate young girls, have been found among their number.

"Not long ago a lady, who was one of the leaders of fashionable society in St. Petersburg, who always appeared at the court balls at the palace, and was the daughter of a very high family, was caught with Nihilistic documents in her possession. Vera Sassulitch, a beautiful girl, who had been well educated, shot the chief of police, General Tepoff, in his own room. She was a Nihilist; and when tried for the offence was acquitted."

To understand the policy of Russia the reader should take the map of Asia and note the sweep of her possessions in the direction of China and India, and recall her efforts to secure the strong military posts in Armenia.

ERZEROUM.

Armenia is one of the most dreary countries in the world. A large part of its population consists of the wandering Kurds, who, like the Arabs, go from place to place, and pitch their tents wherever they find it convenient. Villages are few and far between; and when you reach one, you find it composed of wretched huts, which we should hardly think fit habitations for our domestic animals.

While the upper part of Armenia, extending from the Black Sea to Bayazid, is thus dreary, mountainous, and lonely, the lower portion

FORTIFICATIONS OF TREBIZOND.

of it consists of plains, some of which are smiling and fertile, and are graced with luxuriant vegetation, while other plains are but vast sandy wastes, reminding the traveller of the Arabian Desert. Horses, cattle, and sheep are raised on these plains; and iron and copper are also found in some of them.

The principal towns of Armenia, for military purposes, are Kars,

Trebizond, and Erzeroum. Kars is situated on a height in the midst of valleys, beyond which rise high mountains. Trebizond is the principal Asiatic Turkish seaport on the Black Sea.

Erzeroum stands on a height, as does Kars. Some one who saw this important fortress recently, says of it that, in the distance, "It looks like a large ship thrown ashore under the mountain-side, and its mainmast, distinguishable a great way off, is the tower of the Tepsi minaret." Above the town rise the citadel and fortress. Erzeroum is not a cheerful place. It has poor, unpaved, straggling streets, little tumble-down mud-houses, and is very dirty and slipshod. But it has almost all the curious features of an Oriental town. There are markets and bazaars, baths and fountains, mosques with their bulb-like domes, and more modest churches for the few Christians who dwell there.

In a military point of view, Erzeroum is the most important of all the fortresses in Armenia; and its control by the Russians would give them military command of a country full of places of sacred and historical fame. It is the last defence of the Turks in that part of Asia. If Erzeroum should fall into the full power of Russia, the invaders would find little difficulty of obtaining command of the Euphrates Valley, and may hope to approach Constantinople from that side with little danger of very formidable opposition.

A glance at the map will show what famous places would become a part of the empire of Russia should she succeed in depriving the Sultan of his dominions in Asia.

Palestine and the holy places, with Jerusalem and Bethlehem and Mount Sinai and the banks of the Jordan, would be restored to Christian rule, and the ambition of the Crusaders of the Middle Ages would at last be fulfilled.

Damascus, Smyrna, and Aleppo, famous cities of the Biblical times, and of periods still more remote, would become Russian. The renowned plain and site of ancient Troy would be rescued from the

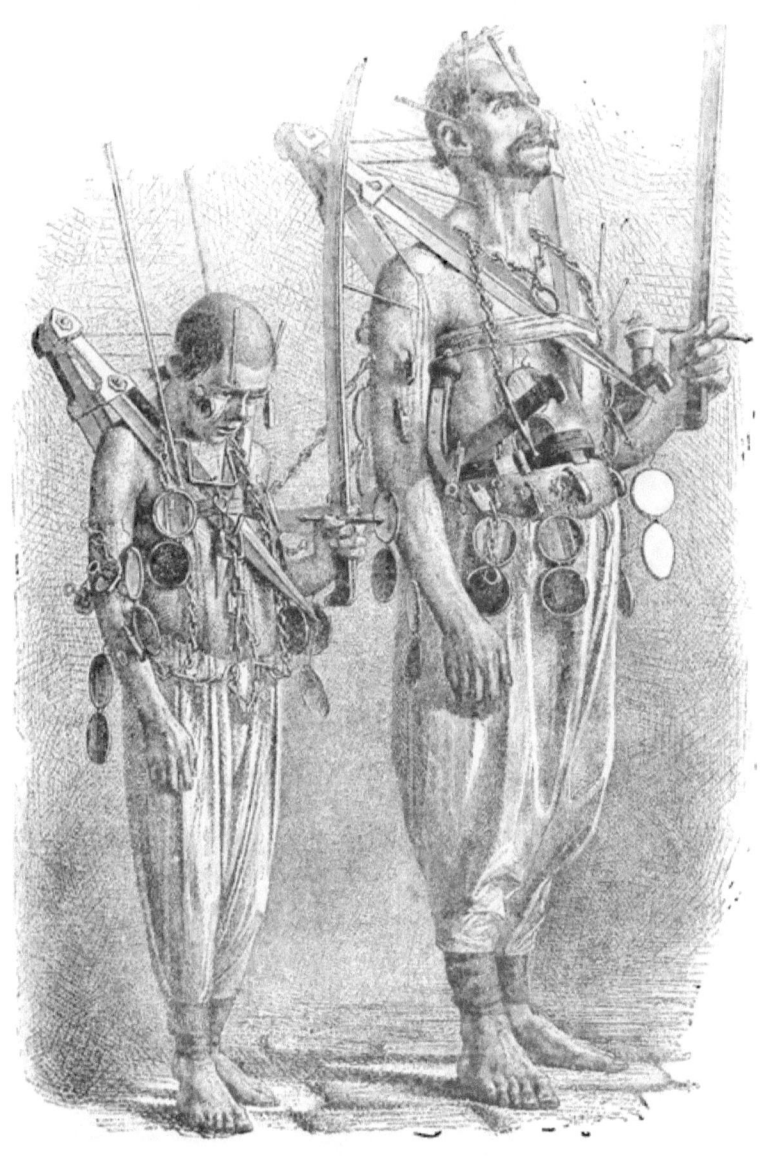

ARMENIAN MARTYRS

Moslem. Bagdad, which no reader of the "Arabian Nights" can forget, for it was the home of the good Caliph Alraschid, and the ruins of the once proud and mighty Babylon, and of the not less mighty Nineveh, would become the possessions of the Czar.

The military and commercial advantages of such a conquest would be very great. The Russians would not only get a footing on the Mediterranean throughout the long line of coast from the Dardanelles to Suez, but would also have access, by the Euphrates Valley, to the Persian Gulf, and by Arabia Petræa to the Red Sea, and thence to the Indian Ocean.

This vast empire Russia covets, and may in time acquire. Russia constantly grows strong, and Turkey weak. The one empire seems to belong to the future, and the other to the past.

We will here relate an amusing old Eastern story; and we hope that, after the explanations we have made, the reader will see the point of it, and how it illustrates the tendency of affairs in the Orient.

THE MISSING SHOES.

A Turkish and a Russian officer once had a dispute about the training and efficiency of their respective soldiers. Each claimed that the discipline of his own army was superior.

"I can prove to you here," said the Russian, "how thoroughly our men are trained."

He called his aide.

"John!"

"Well."

"Go to the bazaar; buy me some tobacco, and return immediately."

The aide saluted him, and turned away as though on a march.

"Now my aide is going to the corner."

"Now he is turning the corner."

"Now he is passing the mosque."

"Now he is at the bazaar."

"Now he is buying the tobacco."

"Now he is coming back.
"Now he is at the door.
"John!"
"Sir."
"Have you the tobacco?"
"*Here*, sir."
The Turkish officer looked coolly on the proceeding, and said, —
"My orderly can do that just as well.
"Muhctar!"
"Well."
"Go to the bazaar and bring me some tobacco. My pipe is out. Instantly, sir.

"Now he is in the street.
"Now he is passing the mosque.
"Now he is stopping to say his prayers.
"Now he is buying the tobacco.
"Now he is coming back.
"Now he is in our street.
"Now he is at the door.
"Muhctar!" exclaimed the officer, in a voice like thunder.
"Sir."
"Have you the tobacco?"
"*I can't find my shoes, sir!*"

The incident of the Czar's secret prayer in the chapel on the night before he issued the proclamation freeing the serfs, which was related by the large-hearted German, so much impressed Wyllys that he made it the subject of a poem, with which we will close the chapter.

THE MIDNIGHT MASS.

It was midnight on the Finland,
    And, o'er the wastes of snow,
From the crystal sky of winter
    The lamps of God hung low.
A sea of ice was the Neva,
    In the white light of the stars,
And it locked its arms in silence
    Round the city of the Tzars.

RUSSIAN MARRIAGE CEREMONY.

THE BLACK SEA.

The palace was mantled in shadow,
   And, dark in the star-lit space,
The monolith rose before it
   From its battle-trophied base.
And the cross that crowned the column
   Seemed reaching to the stars,
O'er the white streets, wrapped in silence,
   Round the palace of the Tzars.

The chapel's mullioned windows
   Are flushed with a sullen light;
Who comes to the sacred altar
   In the silence of the night?
What prince with a deep heart-burden
   Approaches the altar's stair,
To take the wine and the wafer,
   And bow for the help of prayer?

'T is the Tzar, whose word in the morning,
   Shall make the Russias free
From the Neva to the Ural,
   From the Steppe to the winter sea;
Who speaks, and a thousand steeples
   Ring freedom to every man, —
From the serf on the white Ladoga
   To the fisher of Astrakhan.

Oh, faith in Eternal Power!
   Oh, faith in Eternal Love!
Oh, faith that looked up to heaven
   The promise of ages to prove!
The cross and the crown gleam above him;
   He raises his brow from prayer,
The cross of humanity's martyr
   Or crown of the hero to wear.

Slept the serf on the Neva and Volga,
   Slept the fisher of Astrakhan,
Nor dreamed that the bells of the morning
   Would ring in his rights as a man.
He saw not night's crystal gates open
   To hosts singing carols on high,
He knew not a Bethlehem glory
   Would break with the morn in the sky.

The morn set its jewels of rubies
  In the snows of the turret and spire,
And shone the far sea of the Finland,
  A sea of glass mingled with fire.
The Old Guard encircled the palace
  With questioning look on each cheek,
And waited the word that the ukase
  To the zone-girded empire should speak.

The voice of the Russias has spoken;
  Each serf in the Russias is free!
Ring, bells, on the Neva and Volga,
  Ring, bells, on the Caspian Sea!
O Tzar of the North, Alexander,
  Thy justice to those that were least
Shall gird thee with strength of the victor,
  Shall make thee the lord of the East.

CHAPTER XI.

SEBASTOPOL.

THE STORY OF THE CHARGE OF THE LIGHT BRIGADE. — THE STORY OF CATHERINE II. — CEMETERIES. — THE MENNONITES. — "TPRRU."

HE hotel at Sebastopol communicated with the Boulevard, whence a delightful view of the town and harbor could be obtained. The house was formerly the residence of Admiral Nakhimof. The town spreads along the bay, rising gradually to the south; and beyond the houses the ruins of fortifications are everywhere to be seen.

The place was made a great military storehouse by Catherine II.; and she gave the post and port the name, — Sebastopol.

During the first evening's rest at the cool hotel, Master Lewis related to the boys

THE STORY OF THE CHARGE OF THE LIGHT BRIGADE.

The expedition of the Allies to the Crimea was undertaken with the idea that Sebastopol could be taken by a landing, a battle, a march, and an assault. The army landed on the 14th of September, 1854. The battle of Alma followed, which proved disastrous to the Russians; and it was believed in London and Paris that Sebastopol would soon fall.

One of the first efforts of Prince Menschikoff to raise the siege was the advance on Balaclava, which he deemed the weakest point of the defences of the Allies.

It was at the battle of Balaclava. The Russians had surprised the outposts of the Allies, and captured a number of guns. The pride of the British army was the Light Brigade. In the midst of the conflict, Lord Raglan, the British commander, sent the following instructions to Lord Lucan: —

"Lord Raglan wishes the cavalry to *advance rapidly to the front, follow the enemy*, and try to prevent them from carrying away the guns. Troop of horse and artillery may accompany. French cavalry is at your left. Immediate."

These instructions were committed to Captain Nolan, a famous cavalry officer, who seemed to believe that the Light Brigade could sweep over plains of fire and not be vanquished.

Lord Lucan read the order. To obey it seemed to him the destruction of the Light Brigade.

"They are Lord Raglan's orders," said the fiery Nolan, in an authoritative tone.

"What to do?"

Nolan pointed to the valley.

"There, my Lord, is the enemy; and there are the guns."

Here was a mysterious interlude in the battle on the wild plain of the Crimea. An *aide-de-camp* brings instructions to a lieutenant-general to *advance*, and the latter interprets it that he is to *attack* the Russians in their victorious strength, with only eight squadrons of light horse.

"If I do not attack," reasoned Lord Lucan, "I shall be held responsible for the loss of the guns."

Lord Lucan rode over to the Light Brigade.

"Mount," he said. "Attack the Russians in the valley."

"Certainly, sir," said the commander. "But allow me to point out to you that the Russians have a *battery in our front*, and they have *batteries on this flank*, and *batteries on that flank*."

"I cannot help that," said Lord Lucan. "It is Lord Raglan's positive order that the Light Brigade *attacks* immediately."

The valley lay before the Light Brigade, with the dark mouths of guns on every side. A thrill of horror ran through the spectators on the heights when they saw the horsemen, the pride of England, sweep gallantly down into this yawning chasm of certain destruction.

Over the hill, seemingly light as air, they went. Now down, down. There was a rattle of musketry on the heights on one side, — the Fedoukine Heights.

Nolan led bravely. A shell strikes him, ripping open his chest. His shriek is heard even above the uproar. He rides back to the brigade, and drops dead.

CHARGE OF THE LIGHT BRIGADE.

On, on! The guns thunder on the left. The battery in front hisses with tongues of flame. The tramping of the horses' feet go on. Horses fall. Heroes fall. The tempest of hail thickens. The clouds lower on every hand. The Light Brigade grows thinner and thinner. But the ride of death goes on, — on to the end. Six hundred and seventy heroes rode down into that valley and there dealt the enemy a terrible blow; but less than *two hundred* returned. Three hundred and twenty-five horses were mown down, strewing the long, red way.

When Lord Raglan met Lord Lucan he said, —

"You have lost the Light Brigade."

The reader will now be prepared to understand the full import of Tennyson's scenic poem: —

THE CHARGE OF THE LIGHT BRIGADE.

Half a league, half a league,
Half a league onward,
All in the valley of Death
   Rode the six hundred.
"Forward, the Light Brigade!
Charge for the guns!" he said:
Into the valley of Death
   Rode the six hundred.

"Forward, the Light Brigade!"
Was there a man dismay'd?
No, tho' the soldier knew
   Some one had blunder'd:
Theirs not to make reply,
Theirs not to reason why,
Theirs but to do and die:
Into the valley of Death
   Rode the six hundred.

Cannon to right of them,
Cannon to left of them,
Cannon in front of them
   Volley'd and thunder'd:
Storm'd at with shot and shell,
Boldly they rode and well,
Into the jaws of Death,
Into the mouth of Hell
   Rode the six hundred.

Flash'd all their sabres bare,
Flash'd as they turn'd in air,
Sabring the gunners there,
Charging an army, while
  All the world wonder'd:
Plunged in the battery-smoke,
Right thro' the line they broke;
Cossack and Russian
Reel'd from the sabre-stroke
  Shatter'd and sunder'd.
Then they rode back, but not,—
  Not the six hundred.

Cannon to right of them,
Cannon to left of them,
Cannon behind them
  Volley'd and thunder'd;
Storm'd at with shot and shell,
While horse and hero fell,
They that had fought so well
Came thro' the jaws of Death
Back from the mouth of Hell,
All that was left of them,
  Left of six hundred.

When can their glory fade?
O the wild charge they made!
  All the world wonder'd.
Honor the charge they made!
Honor the Light Brigade,
  Noble six hundred!

THE STORY OF CATHERINE OF RUSSIA.

In order that you may understand many things you will see in your journey, you should be made familiar with the story of Catherine, although, I am sorry to say, the personal history of the famous Empress is not a noble one.

She was the daughter of the field-marshal of Prussia and the Princess of Holstein-Gottrop. The Empress Elizabeth of Russia chose her for the wife of her nephew, afterwards Peter III. She came to the Russian Court, united with the Greek Church, and saw with delight an open way for her husband to the throne.

VOLTAIRE.

She dreamed of magnificence, power, a sceptre, and a throne. Her ambitious dreams were at last fulfilled, but not until a fearful tragedy had stained her name forever.

Peter, though royal by birth, was not royal by nature. He was a low, dissolute man. He came to hate the young wife that had been chosen to share his throne; and his affections were given to those who weakened his character and stimulated his bad passions.

Catherine was haughty; and, as her husband chose to associate with bad women, she made favorites of corrupt men. You know how these stories of passion always end in history; and they end in all cases as they do in history. Passion is a sort of volcanic fire; and it ends in explosion at last, and commonly in tragedy.

I will not tell you the story of Peter's favorites or Catherine's lovers; it was all disgraceful. And the cloud that gathered over the unhappy pair grew darker and darker, and sent forth a lightning stroke at last.

In 1762 Peter and Catherine came to the throne. Each hated the other; and one Gregory Orloff was now the lover and favorite of Catherine. Peter resolved to repudiate Catherine; and he formed a plan to arrest and imprison her.

Catherine was full of craft and pride. She had sharp advisers; and she formed a counter plot to dethrone her husband. She committed her cause to her favorite, Gregory Orloff. The people hated Peter for many reasons, both personal and political; and the Court was full of ambitious courtiers, ready for any change that would advance their interests.

Catherine resolved to have her husband arrested and imprisoned, and her son Paul proclaimed Emperor. In this case she would be regent during her son's minority, which would make her in reality the Empress of all the Russias, when she could make and dismiss lovers to her heart's content, and have no one to check her ambition or passion.

Gregory Orloff and his brothers, however, arranged her an even more daring plot. They organized, in secret, a conspiracy among the nobles to proclaim Catherine Empress.

Catherine had been sent away from St. Petersburg. She resolved to return in secret; and the Orloffs arranged that as soon as she entered the city, and was recognized, she should be proclaimed Empress. She started from Peterhof for St. Petersburg in disguise, riding a part of the way in the wagon of a peasant.

Suddenly she presented herself to the National Guards.

"Hail, Empress Catherine!" they exclaimed.

"Arrest the Emperor!" was her first order.

Peter was seized. In a few days the Orloffs went to visit him in his prison. He had a dreadful colic about that time,—such a colic as Arthur of Brittany had when he was visited by King John, and such as the children of Edward had when their Uncle Richard visited them in the Tower. It proved fatal, as these royal and imperial colics usually do; and Peter went to the place where slaves of passion go when tragedy ends all.

Catherine was now Empress, indeed, with a crown on her head and a terrible sin on her heart. She was not happy; but she began her reign by promising the nobles and people everything they desired. She pretended to become pious. She was crowned with great pomp at Moscow; and all the promises she had made to strengthen her throne she now began to fulfil. She reformed the government, strengthened the navy, encouraged industry. The nation grew and prospered; and had the Empress been sure that all her accounts were right in the world above her, she would have been very happy, indeed. Her Courts were full of pleasures and festivities. She put one of her favorites on the throne of Poland, and frightened and humiliated the Turks. She won the Crimea, and added it to the crown.

She now resolved to drive the Turks out of Europe. Over one of the gates of Moscow was written,—"The Way to Constantinople." In the midst of this scheme she made a progress.

It was to the southern and eastern parts of her Empire,—over the territory we are about to visit.

She was now full of pride and power. Her progress was a long triumph. Nothing like it was ever seen. Villages were built where she was to go, to dazzle her for the day. Palaces rose along the dreary wastes, to fade like reflections in the air. False cities were built in the distance, to convey the idea of inexhaustible resources. Masts and flags rose over hills where there were no seas. Bonfires blazed on the evening hills.

She was no longer pious; she espoused the cause of the French philosophers, and welcomed Diderot to her Court; and used to tell him to reveal his whole mind to her, for "among *men*," she said, "no bold belief could cause surprise." But whatever the Empress might say, do, or believe, the memory of Peter's colic must have lain very heavily upon her heart. She invited the crafty infidel Voltaire to her Court, and received the philosopher D'Alembert with great favor.

She began war with Persia, and cherished a scheme for the overthrow of the British power in India. But in the midst of her profligacy and ambition she was suddenly cut off by apoplexy in 1796.

DIDEROT AND CATHERINE II.

Darkness settled over her fame and character; but it was under her reign that the boundaries of Russia were extended to the Black Sea. She visited the Crimea in her day of triumph, and it will always be associated with her name.

The Class visited the English cemetery. It was a desolate place, amid the ruins caused by the war. It consisted of some twenty or more enclosures, where was neither tree nor shrub to remind the visitor of thoughtfulness or affection. The very grasses seemed withered. The nightingale might sing there, were there any green thing to invite or inspire it; but even the bird shuns the barrenness of the place. The graves that dotted the arid soil with an occasional head-stone seemed friendless and forgotten. The plain was desolate, the sky expressionless; and afar rose the tawny mountains without shrub or tree.

Yet here sleep the British heroes of the siege of Malakoff Tower, in whose defence thirty thousand Russians perished; and here the gallant horsemen of the Light Brigade, who rode to death amid incessant mutterings of thunder and hissing tongues of fire.

The coming-on of evening at Sebastopol had its charm, which the Class will long remember. The transparent air, the Caucasian breezes, the Euxine with its white sails, the Tartar boys and girls in the quiet streets, the odd vehicles, the listless, restful aspect of everything in nature and in human life, and even the sense of being amid cities of dead heroes,—all combined to awaken feelings that, in themselves, were unexpressed poems, and reveal how rich in hidden resources is the soul.

One evening there appeared at the inn some people whose serene, spiritual countenances and grave deportment led Wyllys to make inquiry of the landlord about them.

"They are Mennonites," he said.

This stimulated further inquiry; and the boys learned from Master Lewis some interesting facts concerning these people.

The Mennonite Brotherhood is a Christian sect which bears some resemblance both to the Baptists and the Quakers. They are an old sect, and have been influential in Germany for centuries. They are strongly opposed to war, to taking oaths, and to the punishment of death. They are upright and correct in their habits, and very industrious and frugal. Those who have lately emigrated to the United States brought a larger amount of property, in proportion to their numbers, than have any other class of immigrants.

About eighty years ago a large number of German Mennonites were induced by the Czar Paul to settle in Russia. The Emperor was a man of intelligence and of broad views. He knew that the Mennonites were not only a highly moral and religious people, but industrious and thrifty; and he was willing to grant them unusual privileges if they would emigrate to Russia. The charter given by him to the new community provided that neither they nor their descendants should ever be called upon to perform military duty. This privilege induced several thousands of the Mennonites to settle in the Crimea; for not even the Quakers are more opposed to war than are they.

The Emperor Paul honorably kept his word with the Mennonites; and so did his two sons, who successively occupied the throne after his death,—Czar Alexander I. and Czar Nicholas. The Mennonites, left to themselves, became the very best of Russian subjects,—loyal, obedient, quiet, and thrifty. In all the vast territories of the Muscovite Empire there was no locality that, in productiveness and social order, could compare favorably with the district inhabited by these people.

But it seems to be one of the fundamental laws that govern countries, as well as individuals, that prosperity is followed by adversity in one form or another. So far as we can judge, the community of Mennonites did not have within themselves the seeds of disorder and decay. Consequently, the blow at their prosperity came from without.

It is a noteworthy fact that, while this commendable and indus-

CAPTURE OF THE MALAKOFF.

trious colony was upheld and fostered by three of the most warlike monarchs of the present century, all of whom kept faith with the immigrants, it was broken up by one of the most peaceful rulers Russia has ever had. Alexander II. determined to exact military service of the Mennonites in violation of the pledge given by his grandfather.

This decision is causing this inoffensive people to leave Russia as fast as they are able. Of course the Russians, knowing that the Mennonites have greatly enriched the country, are reluctant to have them go, and by all manner of obstacles seek to prevent the exodus. But many have succeeded in getting away, and have already arrived in America.

The Mennonite modes of worship are in wide contrast with that of the clergy of Russia. The one is most simple; the other is ornate and ritualistic, and very splendid in its ceremonies at the time of great convocations.

Tommy sought for stories wherever he went; and he succeeded in securing a very odd one from one of the English-speaking Germans at the inn at Sebastopol. It was a Russian story, — the first that the Class had ever heard.

TPRRU.

There was once a young soldier of Kief, who went to visit his grandfather; and on his way he met an uncommonly handsome girl.

He accosted her somewhat rudely, when she turned to him and said, with a strange look in her eyes, —

"Soldier, you will either break me in the harness, or I will break you!"

What could these mysterious words mean?

He pondered them on his way, and determined to ask his grandfather.

The old gentleman was very wise. He had lived a hundred years and a bit. The soldier related to him the incident that had happened by the way.

The old gentleman listened with surprise, and said, —

"My boy, you know not what you have done. The girl is the daughter of an enchantress. She will come to visit you to-night."

"Well, what am I to do?"

"This. Take a bridle and a whip. In the night she will come running in, and will say, 'Stand still, my steed!' You will then be changed into a horse, and she will drive you over the world, unless you say a secret word."

"What is that word, grandfather?"

"Listen! Your fate depends upon it! The word is TPRRU."

Then the youth said the mysterious word over and over again to himself, — "Tprru, Tprru, Tprru." (We think that the reader will agree that the word is very mysterious; but it is one of good omen. Pronounce it smoothly, and then go on.)

"What will she do," asked the soldier, "when I have said 'Tprru'?"

"She will be turned into a horse."

"And then?"

"Bridle her, and whip her to your liking. She deserves it, the jade."

The soldier followed the old man's advice.

He provided himself with a bridle and whip, and awaited the coming of the enchantress.

At midnight, as the moon was gliding low in the sky, the door suddenly opened.

"Tprru," said the soldier; "Tprru, Tprru, Tprru!"

THE YOUNG SOLDIER.

He opened the door wider, and saw a horse beside the step. He bridled the animal, leaped upon its back, and applied the whip sharply.

He rode the animal into the fields; it tried to throw him. But he had only to say "Tprru" to prevent an accident. It rose in the air, but he said "Tprru," and it came down again. It rushed into the woods, but he needed only to say "Tprru" to prevent the branches of the trees from sweeping him away. As soon as the cocks crew in the morning, the wonderful horse vanished into thin air, and the soldier found himself in his grandfather's house.

RUSSIAN WORSHIP.

"Good-morning, grandfather," he said. "Great is the wisdom you have taught me. One has only to say 'Tprru' to be exempt from all the arts of enchantment."

"You are right, my son; only say 'Tprru,' and you will never be overcome by a witch."

"I think the old man was right, Tommy," said Master Lewis. "Don't forget the word. Just say 'Tprru,' and no witch can ever harm you."

Tommy thought the clever German's story something of a joke. The German was careful not to speak the magic word, but always to spell it in his narrative.

Among the papers that Master Lewis received in a mail at Sebastopol was an American comic journal, containing a little poem on Russian names. He copied this, and, just before leaving the place, sent it to the puzzling German, with his card and compliments.

> "There was a Russian came over the sea,
>   Just when the war was growing hot,
> And his name it was Tjalikavakaree-
>   Karindobrolikanabndarot-
>   Schibkadirova-
>   Ivarditzstova-
>   Sanalik-
>   Danerik-
>   Varagobhot.
>
> "A Turk was standing upon the shore,
>   Right where the terrible Russian crossed,
> And he cried, 'Bismillah! I'm Ab El Kor-
>   Bazaroukilgonautosgobross-
>   Getfinpravadj-
>   Kligekosladli-
>   Grivino-
>   Blivido-
>   Jenidodosk!'"

CHAPTER XII.

THE COSSACKS.

TOMMY MAKES AN ACQUAINTANCE.

HE Class returned to Odessa. The ruins of Sebastopol faded away in the shadowy distance, and the boat glided along over an unruffled sea. Odessa was reached at noon, when all the city seemed in repose; it was like a bright night, for in the midsummer weather the business here is done at morning and evening, and noon witnesses a strange silence in the gay bazaars.

On the following day the Class started on a very zigzag route, as the railroad presented itself on the map, for Moscow.

The Russian railway carriages are made with compartments; they are well, even elegantly, furnished. The trains move slowly, and often stop at a long distance from the town the traveller finds on the map. The distance of many of the stations from the towns whose names they bear, is said to arise from the cheaper rates for which land can be secured a little beyond the suburbs.

The Class passed the first night of their long railway excursion at Elizavetgrad, a city of about twenty-four thousand inhabitants.

"How far are we from Moscow?" asked Tommy, as the train in the evening approached the station.

"Only about 1,071 miles," said Master Lewis.

"*Only!*" repeated Tommy.

The town is situated on a sloping steppe. It has a very wide street, full of shops, and a boulevard, full of acacias. Near the town tumuli were seen, — prehistoric mounds erected by ancient inhabitants.

The second night was passed at Poltava, something more than eight hundred miles from Moscow. It is a larger town than Elizavetgrad. A great fair was just closing here, at which the display of goods had been very great, estimated at more than £3,000,000. People were here from Odessa and from Moscow. The carts about the fair grounds must have numbered many thousand.

The Class was now in the famous land of the Cossacks, — Little Russia, as this part of lower Russia is sometimes called. This part of Russia — on the east side of the Dnieper, and in fact on both sides, without any very definite limits — was known in Poland as the *Ukraine*, in the time of the partitions. Little Russia is made up of the governments of Kiev, Tchernigov, Poltava, and Kharkov.

It was to the Ukraine that the wild horse is related in Byron's poem to have carried Mazeppa.

Jan Mazeppa was born about 1645, and was descended of a noble family in Podolia. He became an officer in the court of Casimir, king of Poland. He insulted the wife of a Polish nobleman, and he was condemned to be stripped naked and bound upon a fiery, spirited horse, lying upon his back, and to be borne away by the frightened animal, and left to his fate. The horse carried him towards the Ukraine. Instead of being killed, as his enemies had intended, he was rescued, joined the Cossacks, and in 1687 was elected their hetman or chief.

The word *Cossack* means robber; it was a name given by the Turks to the predatory tribes inhabiting the banks of the Don. They are famous horsemen, and the council of Russia largely executes the Imperial will by means of the Cossack cavalry.

The journey towards Moscow was by way of the towns of Kharkov,

Belgorod, Kursk, Orel, and Tula. There was a sameness about the route, the scenes, and the inns, that was monotonous, and that became wearisome.

At the Hotel Vienne in Moscow Street, at Kharkov, Tommy met, oddly enough, another good-natured German who could speak English, and he asked him for a story. The German, after thinking for a long time, laid down his pipe and said, —

"I will tell you one tale of Faderland. A Dutch skipper told it me many, many year ago, when I vas in Holland."

We will give the story with amended dialect. We could not produce the original, the half-German, half-English idioms of which were as droll and amusing as the story itself.

"A DUTCH SKIPPER TOLD IT ME MANY, MANY YEAR AGO."

MAZEPPA.

WISH THREE TIMES.

There once was an old couple, with whom life had gone hard. Their children had wandered away from them, and left them alone. Their hair had grown gray. Their means were small; and the winter of age was reducing their accustomed ways of support.

They had lived worthily, and had never complained. The old woman had been a market woman, but she could go into the streets to sell her wares no more.

"Though I am lonely," said the old man, "my son is prosperous beyond the sea. Let us be thankful."

"Though I am lonely," said the old woman, "my young daughter is a bride and lives happy far away. Let us be thankful."

But one day a brother of the old man visited him, and gave him glowing accounts of the comforts that wealth brought to him. Then discontent entered into the old man's heart.

One evening, being alone with his wife by their quiet hearth, he said, —

"Wife, when I was a boy, they used to tell me of fairies that brought good luck to people like us. I wish there were fairies to-day."

Just then appeared a bow of gold in the darkness by the mantel-piece. It was a fairy's wand.

Under it appeared a fairy with silver wings, and a crystal star on her brow.

"Wish three times," said the fairy, waving her wand, "and you shall have your three wishes."

The fairy faded away.

The old couple were greatly surprised; and, when their astonishment was over, became very happy in their dreams of wealth.

"We can wish but three times," said the old man. "We must be very wise."

They talked late by the pleasant fire, considering the subjects of their wishes.

"I am hungry," said the old woman, "and it is getting late. I wish I had a *pudding*."

Immediately on the table before them appeared a pudding.

"Now, see what you have done," said the old man. "You have lost one of your opportunities by your foolish thoughtlessness. It is too provoking. You deserve to suffer for this. I wish that worthless old pudding was fastened to the end of your nose."

Then the pudding, quick as a wink, fastened itself to the end of the old woman's nose, and hung there, a dreadful object to contemplate.

"See what you have done, yourself!" said the old lady, in anger. "We have now but one chance left. We must consider it well."

They considered the matter again. The old lady's nose grew longer and longer under the weight of the pudding, and her sufferings began to be extreme.

"O dear!" she said, "I am very much distressed."

"What?"

"If that pudding was only off my nose I should be happy again."

The pudding fell off.

"Now what have we gained by our three wishes?" asked the old man.

"Nothing," said the old woman.

"We would be wiser if we were to have another chance," said the old man.

But the fairy never came again.

Kursk, a place of some thirty thousand people, is pleasantly situated on the river Tusker. Its numerous gardens constituted its chief beauty to the Class, though there are some twenty stone churches in the town. Orel is a tallow town, as described by its principal industry. Its streets were full of carts of every description; and as the boys here found no one with whom they could converse, they amused themselves wholly with the sights of the streets. The town was founded by John (Ivan) the Terrible, of whom we have, in another chapter, evil stories to tell.

At Orel a young man, evidently a student, entered the compartment of the car in which the Class was travelling. He had a fine face, full of fire and intelligence. As the cars slowly passed on towards Tula, Tommy ventured to address him.

The young man made no answer, but looked at Tommy proudly and rather suspiciously.

"*Ne govoriu po russki*, — I do not speak Russ," said Tommy, using a guide-book phrase, with English accent.

The young man smiled.

FUNERAL OF A POOR RUSSIAN.

"I *do* speak English," he said.

Here seemed a chance for a friendship. Tommy was too lonesome not to improve it.

"You are a Russian," said Tommy.

"Yes, by birth."

"You have a noble — *government*," said Tommy, wishing to continue the dialogue, and hardly knowing what he would say when he commenced the sentence.

"Government?"

"Yes," said Tommy, coloring.

"English people do not often think so."

"Have you travelled in England?" asked Tommy.

"Yes; I have lived in England."

The young man was silent for a long time; and Tommy hardly knew how to frame another question, since the handsome Russian seemed disposed to be unsocial.

At length Tommy engaged in a talk with Wyllys having reference to America.

The young man's face suddenly lighted up, and he asked, with an affable smile, —

"Are you from England?"

"No," said Tommy, "I am from America."

An expression of pleasure passed over the young man's face.

"*You* have a noble government, indeed!" said he. "A government of the people, by the people, and for the people. May it never perish from the earth!"

Tommy was sure that he had heard these sentiments before; in a school declamation, perhaps.

"Are your friends here Americans?" asked the Russian.

"Yes."

"And you like our government?"

"Yes. I like the Czar. Do you not like the Russian government?"

"It certainly differs from yours. Here one man controls the destiny of each of eighty-five million lives. In your country forty million people elect a man to execute their laws, and can change the executive every four years. You have a constitution."

Tommy thought he had studied something about a constitution in history. His ideas were rather vague on the point.

"Has Russia no constitution?" asked Tommy.

"None whatever."

"If you had a bad czar, what would restrain him?" asked Tommy.

"Nothing."

"Who collects the taxes?" asked Tommy.

"The officers of the Czar."

"Who controls the money when it is collected?"

"The Czar."

"Are the taxes heavy?"

"All industries are taxed. The peasant must pay his tax, and help support the great standing army, even if it is an impoverishment to bury his dead and provide a wooden cross for a gravestone."

"Would it not be well for your people to have a constitution?" asked Tommy. "You have a good czar now, and as long as the czar is good the government will be good. But you might have a bad czar at some future time; then what would hinder him from taking your head off?"

"Nothing hinders the present Czar from taking my head off. He could do so if he chose."

"He is absolute," said Tommy. "Have you no Congress or Parliament?"

"We have a Council of State."

"Who elects it?"

"The Czar."

"You have a Senate?" asked Tommy, at a venture.

MILITARY EVOLUTIONS OF THE RUSSIAN ARMY

"Yes, what is called a Senate, but not as you understand the word; its decrees are of no effect, unless sanctioned by the Czar."

"Well, at any rate, you have a very great army?" said Tommy.

"Yes, a very great army, and the Czar taxes the people to support it, — a great army to keep the people in subjection to the Czar, and the people's earnings are taken to pay the price of their own enslavement."

"But why do not the people get together as we do in our country and elect a Congress?"

"If there should be a gathering for such a purpose anywhere in the Empire, every man engaged in it would be sent to Siberia."

"The people could meet in secret and organize," said Tommy.

"The Czar has secret police everywhere. But to meet in secret and organize a government in which the people shall have a voice, and that shall protect every man's rights, is just what the Nihilists are trying to do. If the Czar himself stands in the way of this movement, do you not think he ought to be removed?"

"How?" asked Tommy.

The young Russian made no reply.

There was a long silence. Then Tommy said, —

"Are you a Nihilist?"

"I am for the equal rights of all people before a just code of laws."

The handsome face of the young Russian glowed, and his lip curled, as he uttered this principle. There was a kind of declaration of independence in his very look.

Tommy was thoughtful. At last he said, —

"I would not like to have my life at the mercy of any one man, even if it were the present Czar of Russia, and I do think him one of the noblest men in the world."

"I agree with you, my friend," said the young Russian warmly.

The train stopped at Tula. The young Russian left the compartment, when Master Lewis said to Tommy, in a severe tone, —

"Did you not catch my eye when you were talking to that young man?"

"No."

"Did you not note my silence, and Willys's?"

"I did not think anything at all about it."

"Tommy?"

"Well."

"Don't you ever discuss political matters again with a stranger while you are in Russia."

"Who could have heard us? We were the only persons in the compartment."

"You understand what I have told you?"

"Yes."

Master Lewis went from the car into the station while the train was waiting.

"What makes him speak to me in that way?" said Tommy to Wyllys.

"He suspects that the young man is a Nihilist."

CHAPTER XIII.

MOSCOW.

THE STORY OF IVAN THE TERRIBLE. — THE STORY OF ST. NICHOLAS.

CROWNED in the Cathedral of Assumption, wedded in the Cathedral of the Annunciation, buried in the Church of the Archangel Michael, — such in brief was the history of each of the ancient czars.

The city seems to be all suburbs; and is some thirty miles in circumference. It has nearly twice as many inhabitants as the city of Boston and its suburban towns, — about eight hundred thousand. It all seems built around the Kremlin, which was the old citadel and place of palaces, and which now is a place of treasure-houses and shrines; a monument of the wealth, the pride, and the glory of the past. The streets, in irregular curves, run out from the Kremlin like the spokes of a wheel. The churches are said to number "forty times forty;" the bells of the glimmering domes are almost innumerable; nowhere else on earth is ever heard such music in the air.

The upper air itself seems a glittering city, and the swelling domes often palpitate with the music of bells. When all the bells ring on Easter morn the earth trembles beneath the sound.

The Class approached the city near sunset, when all the domes and crosses seemed on fire.

"Moscow is burning," said Tommy; and so it looked. The cars passed out of fir woods, through levels of rye and barley, and Moscow, blazing on the steppes, appeared, first, like a city of domes in the air, then like a limitless expanse of gilded, silvered, and many-colored cupolas, while high over all were the battlements of the Kremlin.

KRASSNAYA SQUARE.

"The splendor will all vanish when we enter the city," said Wyllys. "It is so in all the places of the East."

"No," said Master Lewis; "you have, I think, reached a city at last that is not illusive in the distance. We shall see."

Master Lewis was right. As the Class on its visit passed through the wide avenues of the city of the steppes, the wonder grew. The

PALACE OF PETROWSKY.

Kremlin, with its palaces, public buildings, and churches; the Petrowsky
Palace beyond the walls; the Red Gate, the Nicholas Gate, Krassnaya
Square, Cathedral Place, the Church of the Protection of Mary, the
Chapel of the Iberian Mother of God, — all of which were duly seen

ST. NICHOLAS CHURCH AND GATE.

and visited, were more wonderfully beautiful when seen close at hand
than under the damask splendors of the late summer sunset. There
were gardens everywhere; most of the roofs were painted green, with
here and there a lordly pomp of Corinthian pillars; gilded stars twin-

kled above the cupolas, and caught the last rifts of the sunlight as the streets grew shadowy.

The Class stopped on Lubianker Street, at a French boarding-house, paying four roubles a day for each, which included bed and board. The houses on the street were much frequented by commer-

CZAR KOLOKOL.

cial men, and among them were a number of Englishmen and several Americans.

The Class first visited the Kremlin, which has grown in grandeur for some five hundred years. The gates of this old citadel are themselves wonderful. They are five in number, in a wall 7,280 feet in circumference. The Gate of the Redeemer is crowned by a picture,

VASSILI-BLAGENNOY (CHURCH OF THE PROTECTION OF MARY).

before which all bow with uncovered heads. Even the Emperor conforms to the custom. Criminals used to be executed before this gate, and made their last prayers to the image. The St. Nicholas Gate, over which is suspended the miraculous figure of the patron saint of Russia, has an imposing tower, and we give a view of it here. Within

GRANOVITAYA PALATA

the walls and gates of the Kremlin are the most historically interesting buildings of the city, the most sacred places, the remains of the ancient palaces, and the tombs of the czars.

The Class first ascended the tower of Ivan (John), 325 feet high, where they saw suspended thirty-four bells, the largest of which weighs sixty-four tons. The highest of these bells are silver. From this tower the magnificence of the Kremlin, and the surprising extent of the city, were seen. Paying the *custode* fifty copecks to show the wonders of the Kremlin, the Class were next taken to view the Great Bell — the Czar Kolokol — at the foot of the tower. It is large enough for a chapel, and weighs 444,000 pounds. It is nineteen feet high, and sixty feet in circumference. The Class visited the Gold Court of the Palace, from whose stairs the czars of old used graciously to allow the populace to see the "light of their eyes," but not the wickedness of their hearts. It was on the same stairs that John the Terrible saw the comet, and trembled at the sight, like Belshazzar at the writing on the wall; and here also he struck his spear through the foot of a messenger, who brought him unwelcome news, and pinned him to the floor. The Granovitaya Palata, the old hall of coronation banquets, was next seen. We give a view of its entrance. In the Treasury — a sort of second Tower of London, though a modern structure — were seen jewels innumerable.

The Class on the second day in the city visited the Church of Assumption, on the platform of whose nave the czars have been crowned. In this church is shown a picture of the Virgin, which is said to have been painted by St. Luke. The jewels with which it is adorned are valued at £45,000. Here also is the silver shrine of St. Philip, a prelate who dared to condemn the crimes of Ivan the Terrible, and who became a martyr for his zeal and fearlessness.

In the morning, before leaving the hotel to visit this historic church, Master Lewis related to the boys the story of the life of

IVAN THE TERRIBLE.

Ivan (or John), called the Terrible, showed his brutal instincts when a mere boy. It is related that he used to sit in a lonely tower and delight himself in torturing harmless animals; and certain it is that at the age of thirteen he ordered his guards to have one of the chiefs of the government torn in pieces by hounds. At his coronation he took the title of czar. He conquered Kazan, and won the kingdom of Astrakhan. He waged war with Livonia, and with increase of power grew also the strength of his enemies in court and camp. He surrounded himself with a guard called "The Thousand of the Czar." The head

THE RED GATE.

of a dog was the emblem of this body of men, and was supposed to signify that each man was ready to bite any enemy of the Terrible Ivan.

He now began to punish traitors; and the slaughters he caused filled the land with horror. His brutal passions grew with each bloody revenge. He had absolute power, and could destroy men or even towns at will. Among other acts he "chastised" Novgorod, which chastisement consisted of the slaughter of, according to one historian, some sixty thousand persons.

"Men say I am cruel," he said. "I am; I do not deny it. But to whom am I cruel? I am cruel to those who are cruel to me. The good, — ah, I would give them the chain and robe I wear!"

He had many compunctions of conscience, and used to ask the monks to pray for the *souls* of his victims, before and after his inhuman slaughters.

After twenty-five years of success in wickedness a change came. He lost his Western conquests, his three wives died, and a most frightful disease fastened itself upon him.

His hope was in his son; he loved him, as brute may love its young. But one day he had a dispute with him, and his anger, after a growth of a life-time, could not be restrained. He dealt him a dreadful blow, and the youth fell dead.

Then horror filled his mind. He had destroyed his own work. He had no successor, and enemies arose on every hand. After three years of darkness and fear and hopeless grief he died, having experienced in his last years as poignant sufferings as he had inflicted on others.

St. Philip, whose shrine we are about to visit, was a man bold and conscientious enough to arraign this dark Czar for his crimes. One day, after Ivan had caused many of the nobles to be put to death, and had devastated many towns near Moscow, the people entreated Philip to make an appeal for them. Philip forbade the Czar to attend mass. But at a solemn service the Czar appeared, and with him a body of profane and obnoxious men.

"The Czar demands thy blessing," said these rude followers to Philip.

Then the prelate, fearing no power but God, faced the Czar.

"Why hast thou come here, where the offering to God is a bloodless sacrifice, — thou with thy blood-stained hands?"

"Seditious monk," said Ivan, in rage. "I am only too merciful to traitors. I will now be what you have called me."

"Silence," said Philip to the Czar, nobly, on one occasion; "silence lays sins upon the soul. I am a stranger and a pilgrim upon the earth, as all my fathers were, and I am ready to suffer for the truth."

Ivan at last caused the old man to be driven from the altar and put into prison. He executed his relatives and friends; and once sent him the head of his beloved nephew, with the message, "Dost thou recognize it?" The saint blessed it and kissed it. He was executed; but his memory is held in the highest esteem in Russia. It is one of the customs of the emperors to kiss his relics.

It was of Ivan that Mrs. Hemans wrote the familiar poem beginning, —

> He sat in silence on the ground,
>   The old and haughty Czar,
> Lonely, though princes girt him round,
>   And leaders of the war ;
> He had cast his jewelled sabre,
>   That many a field had won,
> To the earth beside his youthful dead,
>   His fair and first-born son.

ST. NICHOLAS.

The name of St. Nicholas appears everywhere in Russia.

St. Nicholas lived over fourteen hundred years ago in the city of Patara, in Asia Minor. He is said to have been a saintly child; and when he became a man, though he was but a simple citizen, he rose, through his active piety, to be Bishop of Myra. Wonderful stories are related of his good deeds, and some of them are commemorated to this day in the various churches of Europe.

A wealthy gentleman in Asia, we are told, once sent his two sons to Athens to be educated. He charged the boys at parting to stop at Myra on their way and pay their respects to his reverence, the bishop. The boys reached the city at night, and took lodgings in an inn, intending to make the promised call in the morning.

Now the landlord was a very wicked man, and when he saw their rich store of baggage he resolved to rob and murder his guests. So, when the poor boys were asleep, he crept up to their room and despatched them ; and, to conceal his terrible deed, he cut up their bodies and packed them in a pickling-tub with some pork, intending to sell the whole to some ship in the Adriatic.

Now good St. Nicholas that night saw it all in a dream ; and in the morning he put on his pontifical robes (for he was now an archbishop), and, with his crozier in his hand, went in holy indignation to the inn.

The landlord was greatly frightened when he saw the archbishop, and, on being accused, fell upon his knees and confessed his crime.

St. Nicholas next went to the tub in all his pontificals ; and he passed his hands over the boys, who at once hopped up out of the pickled pork, alive and whole. The happy fellows began to sing praises to St. Nicholas, but he, good soul, would not listen to it. He told them to worship none but God. The boys, at once recovering their possessions, went on their way rejoicing ; and St. Nicholas was regarded as the special protector of boys and students from that hour.

Most of the old pictures represent three boys in the pickling-tub, all with uplifted hands, praising good St. Nicholas. We suspect that three boys in the tub, instead of two, better suited the fancy of the old artists. It did not make a great deal of difference in point of fact, and it certainly made a better picture.

"But how came St. Nicholas to be the patron of Christmas gifts and the particular saint of the Christmas holidays?"

After St. Nicholas was made archbishop at Myra he became very rich; and because he despised money for its own sake, he spent a good portion of his time in giving away his money to others, and in such a way that none should know from whom it came. It chanced that there was a very poor nobleman in Myra, who had three lovely daughters. Knowing that they could have no marriage portion, St. Nicholas, considerate soul! felt pity for them; and one moonlight night he took a purse, round as a ball with gold, and throwing it into the open window at the feet of the eldest daughter, he hid himself from view. The eldest daughter could now marry. What a good saint St. Nicholas was, and what a pity he died so long ago! After a while the saint visited the nobleman's premises again, and did the same mysterious kindness to the second daughter. The nobleman now began to keep watch at night, in order to discover whence his sudden good fortune came. As good St. Nicholas was about to throw another rounded purse at the feet of the third daughter, he was discovered by the grateful father, who threw himself at his feet, saying, "O St. Nicholas, servant of God, why seek to hide thyself?"

St. Nicholas made the nobleman promise never to tell the discovery he had made; but the secret escaped in some unaccountable way; and after St. Nicholas died, the nuns of the convents in the East imitated him on certain holidays in making secret gifts to their friends. They used to put silk stockings at the door of the abbess at night, and label them with a paper, invoking the liberal aid of good St. Nicholas. In the morning the stocking would be found full of presents.

In time, as you know, children began to imitate this custom, especially at Christmas.

St. Nicholas used annually to be honored in the old English churches by the election of a boy-bishop, whom the whole Church were accustomed to obey for a short time, because St. Nicholas was the patron of boys. He is still honored with a grand festival at Bari on the Adriatic; is the patron saint of Russia, and of the mariners on the great winter seas; and his name is borne by the Russian czars. Of all saints he is most reverenced in Holland. He is also the patron saint of New York City, which, you know, was settled by the Dutch.

CHAPTER XIV.

NIJNI NOVGOROD.

The Wonderful Fair at Nijni Novgorod.

THE empire of Russia covers nearly one twenty-fourth of the surface of the whole globe, and more than one sixth of the land surface. Its principal trade is done in summer.

Nijni Novgorod is its market place.

The merchants gather here from all Eastern lands; indeed, some of the Asiatic travellers spend two thirds of the year in their journeys to and from Nijni. Here sunny Persia unfolds her gaudy fabrics, and dark Siberia the barren products of her steppes, forests, and hills. Hither China sends her tea in Russian caravans; here Tartars of all types are seen, and showmen from every province.

In early summer there is a horse fair here, where the finest animals of the steppes are exhibited. Russia is famous for her fine horses, especially Lower Russia or the Ukraine. In the winter a local fair is here held on the ice of the Volga. People come to it in sledges.

The Great Fair is formally opened on the 15th of July. The officers of the government and town then march from the cathedral with crosses and banners, and cross the bridge of the Oka. The priests bless the waters and pray for the empire; then the flags of the nation are thrown to the breeze, and the Fair is declared to have begun.

There is little trade at this time. For weeks all is preparation. On the 25th of July, the Festival of St. Makarius, the archbishop, with an imposing procession, marches around the Fair.

Trade now begins. The tea is sold. About the 10th of August the traffic in all commodities is at its height. Hundreds of thousands

RUSSIAN SLEDGES.

of people come and go in an endless throng, like a world's caravan. Mounted Cossacks flit hither and thither on fleet horses, trying to keep order. The fashion and wealth of St. Petersburg and Moscow flow into the human sea like a golden tide. The gypsies come flocking to the town from places of which little is known to history or civilization. From the 10th to the 25th of August the Fair is the theme, the life, and the pride of Russia.

The Class reached Nijni about the 20th of the month.

What a Fair!

One who has heard the common expression, "It is the greatest Fair in the world!" is led to expect wonderful sights. He is at first disap-

A COSSACK.

pointed; then the magnitude of the commerce becomes an astonishment.

A succession of wharves running along the Oka and the Volga ten miles in length!

Goods piled upon them until they look like hills!

The Siberian wharf a mile in length!

The tea on this wharf, packed in bales and covered with matting, forms alone a surprising elevation nearly a third of a mile in length!

The teas to be used in the Russias for a whole year are here. The people who protect the bales live in huts of matting, and are in themselves a colony. The carts for the transportation of these goods would form a procession of miles.

The mountains of tea are not the only wonders.

Here are enormous masses of iron from the Oural. There are valleys of iron. Hills of tea and valleys of iron.

In the town is a crowd of all peoples of the East. The sun is a blaze of splendor. The Volga flows calmly by.

Such is Nijni!

At this time the number of visitors must have been from 150,000 to 200,000 daily. Goods had been sold to the value of nearly one hundred millions of roubles, of which a large portion was tea and iron. It was estimated that £15,000,000 were in circulation.

Nijni is a town of churches as well as traffic and shows. There are some fifty-eight houses of worship in the place. One of these, called the Nativity of Our Lady, built in 1719, is painted in the colors of the rainbow. The population of the town or city at other times than the Fair is only about forty thousand.

The town is divided into two parts, the old and the new. It is built on hills, and overlooks the great rivers of the Volga and Oka. The fortress or Kremlin, with its white crenellated walls, stands like a guard over all; and the old town reposes as if in its shadow.

The Class took rooms at the Hotel de Russie, near the Kremlin, paying each about ten shillings a day. Englishmen, Frenchmen, and people who spoke English or French or both, were at once met, and, after their long and rather monotonous journey, the boys began to have a home feeling again.

After a night's rest Master Lewis and the boys started out to take their first view of the Fair. They hired a droshky boy, with a little Tartar horse, to take them to the Tower of Mouravieff, — so named from the governor who built it. The little horse tugged heroically at his collar up the steep hill.

The wonderful extent of the Fair appeared as they ascended; and from the top of the tower they surveyed the whole scene of the great Eastern market place.

A huge plain lay before them, flanked by two rivers, and covered with picturesque houses, or dwellings, of brick, wood, and straw, of red, white, and yellow. Over this plain piles of merchandise appeared in every direction. Church spires rose above this summer city; mosques, playhouses, and bright flags.

The two rivers, as far as the eye could see, were full of barges. The miles of wharves were scenes of the liveliest activity. Beyond the town were the faubourgs of the Fair, stretching as far as the eye could see.

A DROSHKY BOY.

The boys used their glasses, and swept these vast faubourgs, covered with tea, iron, hides, and heavy merchandise.

They then descended and followed one of the streets to the faubourgs.

Everywhere were cheap eating-houses, where one might obtain a meal of cabbage-soup, meat, and black bread for eight copecks (about six cents).

Under ground were stone cisterns of water, as a protection against fire; and passages connecting them, into which one might go to smoke, — in fact smoking at the Fair is not permitted *above ground* at all.

Tea was the leading commodity. The Russians are famous tea-drinkers; and every leaf of tea used in the vast empire was once brought first to Nijni, and largely comes in this way still.

The manner of tea-drinking in Russia is peculiar. The Russian uses a piece of lemon in his cup instead of cream. He puts a lump of sugar in his mouth, instead of in his cup, before drinking; and sometimes eats the leaves of tea after the cup is drained. Perhaps some of our readers may like to make an experiment of tea-drinking in this way, using the bit of lemon for cream, and taking the sugar into the mouth just before drinking. Tommy tried it, and liked it.

To Tommy the crowning glory of the Fair, so far as merchandise went, was watermelons.

In their journey to Moscow the boys had found fine melons at nearly every station.

"Russia is the land of sunflowers and watermelons," said Tommy. "I never was able to find as many melons as I wanted before."

It is impossible to convey any adequate impression of the variety of goods; the gold and silver smiths' shops, the magnificent wares of the haberdashers, the curious wonders in shell and wood, the furniture, the millinery, the splendid rugs and carpets, the fruit-stores, bazaars for fancy articles, and the *cafés*.

The gypsies of Northern Europe are always found at great fairs. Fairs are their gala days, and they flock to Nijni. The Russian gypsies that roam over the steppes, loving the scowling sky, and the hardship of baffling cutting winds and drifting snows, are wholly unlike the olive-hued, guitar-playing wanderers of Italy and Spain, but weird and wild in their type. They at once suggest Scott's picture of Meg

NIJNI NOVGOROD DURING THE FAIR.

Merrilies. In contrast with these restless travellers were the Cossacks, from the dark lagoons and green fields of the Don. The Cossack children were particularly interesting, with a certain beauty, intelligence, and vivacity in their strongly marked features that drew the eye of the stranger after them wherever they appeared.

The Fair of Nijni Novgorod, beside being the great centre of exchange for Asiatic and European commodities, is also the great pleasure resort — the summer play-house — of the East.

As evening comes on, myriad lights glimmer in the streets along the Oka; colored lanterns begin to transform the scene; music is heard everywhere; the tired Asiatics lie down to sleep in their barges or on their bales of goods; then the Europeans drop business and give themselves up to diversion, each according to his taste.

INHABITANT OF NIJNI NOVGOROD.

Amusement-seeking, for any other purpose than needed change, relaxation from work, mental rest, does not tend to morality and virtue; a true man seldom courts amusement for its own sake, but finds his enjoyment in his business, object in life, duty. The general reputation of the amusements at the Fair used to be bad, when drinking, carousing, unseemly dancing, made a riot of the night.

The Fair has greatly improved in this respect during the present decade. The nights are orderly. The merchants banquet, the small traders drink tea. Card-playing is common. Musicians here, as in all places in Russia, are the popular entertainers. There are concerts everywhere, and of all grades, even far out in the faubourgs.

A RUSSIAN GYPSY.

The Theatre Bouffe was filled with a rough crowd. Mademoiselle Froufrou was dancing her pranks and singing her ditties, in very scant clothing, and the audience cheered her tremendously.

"Five minutes here will do," said Master Lewis. "I think I have seen enough already."

"Wait a little," said Tommy. "Let me see her *caper.*"

"Would you like to have a sister of yours *caper* in that way?"

"A *sister*, — no; I would never speak to her again as long as I lived."

"And I do not care to see some one's else sister caper, — we will go."

The theatre devoted to the legitimate drama was only partly filled. The people here were evidently respectable and intelligent well-to-do merchants of European cities.

The Class could not understand the play; but one scene representing three gypsyish women making incantations around a caldron was weird and entertaining.

"I think it is *Macbeth*," said Master Lewis.

The Class next went to the door of one of the smaller play-houses.

CARD-PLAYING IN BARGES ON THE VOLGA.

There was music within. Master Lewis entered in advance of the boys. He opened an inner door, and stopped a moment.

"*That* will do," he said. "We will go."

Tommy found the "Turks, Jews, and gypsies" at the Fair as he

THE THREE WITCHES IN THE CAVE.

had anticipated, but he was unable to hold conversation with them; they were all like people on exhibition to him. He presented the palm of his hand to one little gypsy woman, who had long braided hair and snakish eyes, to have his fortune told. She examined the hand carefully, then leaped to her feet, and pointed upward in a very theatrical way, uttering exclamatory sentences that Tommy could not understand.

"She has discovered something wonderful about me!" said Tommy. "I wish I knew what it is."

Soon after leaving her, Tommy made a discovery: his watch was missing! He went back to find the woman, but she was gone. His faith in her prophetic visions was not stimulated by this disclosure.

A BULGARIAN BEGGAR.

"She evidently did discover something wonderful about you," said

Master Lewis. "I am afraid that she will never go in the direction she pointed."

There were many Tartars at the Fair, — women and men, — in costumes seen only in the East. Beggars were there, of all descriptions; mendicant monks, and even tramps from Bulgaria and the Turkish provinces, who had reached there somehow, — possibly by way of the Volga.

BEARS IN A SIBERIAN VILLAGE.

There were mosques there as well as churches; and there also, as in Turkey, the Mohammedans were seen bowed in prayer.

Among the street shows that most interested Tommy were the performances of some tame bears from Siberia. No one seemed to fear them more than as though they were dogs. On inquiring about these bears, he was told that they belonged to a species so tame and harmless that they sometimes appeared in the streets of Siberian villages, and were driven about like domestic animals, sometimes even to market.

The Fair at Nijni is losing its importance; the railroad system of Russia is distributing trade. As a gay gathering of Russian merchants, a great summer festival, it will soon be a bygone glory; but the iron from the Ourals will long continue to be brought here; and a great city, looking down on the Volga from the cool hills, will gradually take the place of the Fair.

The Class spent their last evening in one of the tea rooms, where a band of Russian singers and a middle-aged story-teller — evidently the father of the girls who furnished the music — entertained the guests. The boys were pleased with the singing, but could not understand the story. Tommy, however, learned the substance of it afterwards from an English-speaking family who were present from the hotel. It was a popular Russian tale, and one especially pleasing to girls. We give it in our own language here. The Russian entertainer called it "Vasilissa the Fair," but we will give it another title, more practical and less Oriental in its suggestions.

THE STORY OF THE DOLL THAT SPOKE.

In one of the fairest provinces of the East there lived a merchant. He had a lovely wife and a beautiful daughter. The wife was suddenly taken ill, and the doctor told her that she must die.

She called her little daughter to her bedside, and said, —

"Vasilissa, I am going away. I give you my blessing; may it protect you in the hour of evil. With my blessing I leave you this doll. Keep it always with you, and never let any one see it. It is a wonderful doll. It can speak. Whenever any misfortune comes upon you, give it food to eat, and ask its advice. When it has fed it will tell you how to escape from misfortune, and will help you to perform any service you may need."

Then the poor woman kissed her little girl, and died.

In time the merchant married a widow who had daughters of her own, and the woman and her daughters began to treat Vasilissa very ill.

Now Vasilissa was the prettiest girl in the province, and many young men of noble birth and character came to seek her hand.

But her envious step-mother said, —

"Vasilissa shall never marry until I have married my own daughters. They are older than she, and it is not fitting that the youngest should marry first."

Then she set Vasilissa to do the work in the garden and kitchen, hoping she would become tanned by the sun and wind, and would lose her queenly grace by drudgery.

But whenever she was left alone, Vasilissa would take the beautiful doll from her pocket, and say, —

> "Little dolly, feed!
> Help me in my need!"

Then the doll would eat and comfort Vasilissa and perform for her all the work she had been set to do. She would weed the garden while Vasilissa sat in the cool shade of the trees; she would wash the dishes while Vasilissa listened to the birds that came to sing to her in the rose-bushes by the lattice.

One summer the merchant must needs go to foreign lands. He removed his family to a summer-house in a great forest, and left them there. Here, as elsewhere, Vasilissa was set to do the hard work; but the doll helped her, and she always looked like a beautiful lady, and not like a slave.

Now, in the forest, not far from where the merchant's family lived, there was a lonely hut; and in it lived a very wicked old woman, whom all persons shunned and feared. It was said that many people who had gone to visit her from time to time were never seen again, nor did any searching of the foresters reveal what had become of them.

The jealous step-mother ordered Vasilissa several times to go to the hut of the wicked old woman and borrow things of which there was need in the kitchen.

But Vasilissa did nothing without consulting the doll. And as often as she said, —

> "Feed, dolly, feed!
> Help me in my need!"

and asked if she should go to the hut of the old woman to borrow, the doll replied, "Do not go; the woman is a Baba Yaga!"

Now a Baba Yaga means a scolding old woman, a fault-finder; but it was also applied to dangerous people, who are suspected of destroying life.

Autumn came. The leaves turned crimson, gold, and russet, and the wind rustled mournfully among them at evening, and the forests began to lose their bird songs, and to be dreary and lone. The weather grew cold, and the evenings long.

One day the fire went out in the house, towards evening.

"Never mind," said the merchant's wife, "we have still a lighted candle, and before that burns down we will rekindle the fire."

She set her daughters and step-daughter to work,—one of them to making lace, one to knitting socks, and Vasilissa to weaving. Then she fell asleep in her chair.

At last the candle needed snuffing; and one of the girls took the snuffers, and thinking to do the work thoroughly, snuffed out the candle.

The merchant's wife awoke.

"What have you done?" said she.

A BABA YAGA.

"Snuffed out the light," said one of the girls.

"What are we to do?" said she. "We have no light nor fire. We must send to the Baba Yaga for a light."

"My pins give me light enough," said the lace-maker. "Let Vasilissa go."

"My knitting-needles give me light enough," said the other daughter. "Let Vasilissa go."

"Vasilissa," said the mother, "go to the Baba Yaga's, and borrow a light."

Vasilissa went to her room in the dark, and gave the doll some food.

"Feed, dolly, feed!
Help me in my need!"

Then the doll said,—

"Go to the Baba Yaga's; I will protect you."

Out into the cold, under the light of the round moon, went Vasilissa to the Baba Yaga's.

The way was long and dreary; but at last she saw under the branches of some tall trees the light in the hut of the Baba Yaga.

She went to the door and knocked.

"Faugh! faugh! who is there?"

"It is I, Granny. My step-mother has sent me to borrow a light."

"I know her well. Come in."

She went in and found the Baba Yaga sifting poppy-seed through her fingers, clearing it from dirt, grain by grain.

"It is slow work, Granny," said Vasilissa. "It must take a long time to sift a measure full. If you will get me a light I will help you."

The old woman went into another room as if for a light and a lantern.

Then Vasilissa said, —

"Feed, dolly, feed!
Help me in my need!"

and she gave the doll a bit of cake, and in a twinkling all the poppy-seed was sifted and changed from one measure to the other.

Presently the Baba Yaga said, —

"Little maiden, come here, and see what you will see."

Then the doll said, —

"Stay where you are."

"No, Granny, come here; I have sifted the seed."

The Baba Yaga came back looking very fierce.

"How did you sift the seed so quickly?"

"I do all my work quickly."

"How?"

"My mother's blessing assists me."

"Have you been blessed?"

"Yes; my mother blessed me, when dying, in the name of God."

"Then I cannot harm you. This is no place for blessed people. Here is a lantern, — go, — go, — and never come here again!"

As Vasilissa was returning with the light she met the prince of the country. As soon as he saw her he fell in love with her, and took her to the royal palace and married her. She made a good queen, and one greatly beloved, because she always, in trouble, consulted the doll which she carried in her pocket. They called her Vasilissa the Fair; and her life was as beautifully crowned with graces as her head with the jewels of the diadem.

CHAPTER XV.

ST. PETERSBURG.

St. Petersburg. — The Relations of Greece to the Eastern Question. — A Strange Incident. — Story of Peter the Great.

"I THINK I now fully understand the Eastern Question," said Tommy, as the train moved away to Moscow, "except in one point."

"What is that?" asked Master Lewis.

"The relation of Greece towards Turkey and the European Powers."

"It is very simple and natural. The Turks, about the year 1355, made themselves masters of Thrace, Macedonia, Thessaly, and afterwards enslaved the whole of Greece. Now that Turkey is becoming weak, and that Greece is growing strong, and has already recovered a large part of her ancient dominion, she naturally aims to secure the whole of it, and to be what she was in the days of prosperity and power.

"When Greece became independent of Turkey, about fifty years ago, and after many centuries of bondage was formed once more into a free nation, there still remained, and have remained to this day, certain provinces inhabited by Greek populations, under the rule of the Sultan. The principal of these provinces lie in the ancient Greek States of Thessaly and Epirus, both of which border on the frontiers of the present Greek kingdom, and whose people ardently desire to join the federation of their Greek fellow-countrymen. The old historic city of Janina is included in this region, and the Greeks are especially eager to annex it to their realm.

"When the Russo-Turkish war broke out in 1877, the Greeks thought they saw their opportunity to obtain these provinces, and prepared to join in the war against the Sultan. But they were urged to desist from hostilities by the European Powers, and were encouraged by these Powers to expect some of the coveted territory at the end of the war, as the price of keeping the peace.

"Such an intention was inserted in the Treaty of Berlin; but up to this day the hope of the Greeks has not been realized.

"The present King of Greece is in full sympathy with the ambition of the country. He is the son of the King of Denmark, who a few years ago was one of the most obscure of the European princelets. The Greeks chose him for their king.

"One of his sisters is the Princess of Wales, who will probably ere long be the Queen of England.

"Another sister is the wife of the czarowitz, and may soon be Empress of Russia. (She is now the Empress.)

"From this situation it would seem that Greece, in her future struggles with Turkey, — and she is certain to revive these struggles until she recovers her traditional boundaries, — would be likely to have the sympathy of the royal folks in England and Russia."

"The poor Turks!" said Tommy, with mock gravity.

The Class stopped in Moscow a single day, during which a surprising incident occurred.

Hearing that a band of exiles was to be taken to Siberia, Master Lewis obtained permission of the officers to visit them in prison. Permission was not obtained for the boys.

When he returned to the hotel he said, —

"I have seen a sight to make one's heart ache. The condemned men are Nihilists. Among them was an old man who was exiled some years ago, but returned home to see his family, and was discovered. I pitied his gray hairs. And among them also was a very handsome young man, with irons on his feet. Who do you think it was?"

"It could not be any one that we have known," said Tommy.

CONVICTS ON THEIR WAY TO SIBERIA.

"It was the very young man you talked so freely with on the way to Moscow."

"How did he appear?"

"Proud, cold, and indifferent."

"Is the Russian Government as hard and despotic as he represented?"

"I think not, except in the matter of disloyalty to the Czar.

"It is generally thought that Russia is a vast and absolute despotism, ruled over by a single autocratic will; and that the Russian people, having no voice in their own affairs, have nothing to do but to obey the mandates of the Czar.

"While it is true that the Russian monarch is absolute, and Russia is the only nation in Europe which does not have a general Parliament to make its laws and restrict the power of the sovereign, it is an error to suppose that the people have no voice in their political, or, at least, their local, affairs.

"The peoples' power lies in the very peculiar and interesting organization of the Russian villages. Russia, indeed, may be called a nation of villages. It contains very few large cities; and throughout that vast country, comprising nearly one half of the entire continent of Europe, there are only about one hundred and fifty towns whose population exceeds ten thousand.

"All over that wide extent, however, are clustered the villages which contain the bulk of the Russian people. Far from being sparsely settled, as many think, European Russia contains as many people to the square mile as that part of our own country which lies east of the Mississippi River. The country is fairly dotted with busy little communities, which have their own customs and institutions, and are quite distinct from large towns."

"How are these villages governed?"

"That is what I was about to explain.

"Not by agents and mayors sent from St. Petersburg to rule them, but by their own free votes and action.

"The Russian village elects not only its own executive officers, but its own judges. It has its local Legislature, elected every three years, in which nobles and peasants sit together as equals. Great landed proprietors and their former serfs are to be seen side by side in this body; and the vote of the serf is as good as that of his former master.

"There is a yet more curious fact in relation to these self-governing villages of autocratic Russia. They are one and all corporations, which hold the entire land on a perpetual lease; and each inhabitant owns, not a plot of land, but all the land, in common with his neighbors. The land is parcelled out among the villagers, not to own, but to cultivate; and the products of the fields belong, not to the man who raises them, but to the village which disposes of them. Then the vil-

VILLAGE ON THE ROUTE TO ST. PETERSBURG.

lage, as a corporation, maintains and supports all the inhabitants, pays the taxes to the General Government, and provides for the poor and helpless.

"In this journey I have tried to instruct you, not only in the political affairs, but in the history of Russia. I have, in stories told in association with places, given you views of the lives of the great rulers, except Peter the Great. The journey from Moscow to St. Petersburg

— the city of Peter — will be long and uninteresting. I shall try to make it more pleasant, and to prepare your minds for the visit to the Russian capital, by relating some stories of this strange, resolute, and powerful man."

The route from Moscow to St. Petersburg was indeed uninteresting, — a twenty hours' dreariness, a sameness of 403 miles. It is said that when the engineers disagreed about a route for the railroad, the Czar settled the question by drawing on a map before him a straight line from St. Petersburg to Moscow. One who passes over the route will readily believe the story.

The road was built by the government. The principal stations are handsome, and well supplied with refreshments; but the long distances between them present few picturesque views to the stranger.

A SAD STORY OF PETER THE GREAT.

Peter the Great, the upbuilder of the Russian Empire, was born in Moscow, June 9, 1672. During his minority the grand-duchess Sophia, an ambitious, crafty, and withal terrible woman, acted as regent. She was his half sister. He was obliged to rebel to depose her from the throne, a seat which she greatly liked; but he at last obtained the imperial power, and shut her up in a convent.

Peter was a far-seeing man; he had some great virtues, but was naturally brutal, sensual, and passionate. Once, when he was absent from the country, the Guards rebelled and joined a conspiracy to place Sophia again on the throne. Peter, hearing of the plot, hurried back to Moscow, crushed the rebellion, and caused some two thousand of the Guards to be beheaded.

He was so enraged at this revolt that he cut off many of the heads of the condemned men with his own hand. At one time, while half intoxicated at a banquet, he ordered twenty of the prisoners to be brought into the hall, and caused them one by one to be laid upon the block for him to execute. He took a glass of brandy after each execution. In an hour he had cut off the heads of twenty men.

Peter kept a jester to lighten his heavy spirits, and no monarch ever more needed the stimulant of cheerfulness to make him a merciful man. The jester's name was Balakireff.

One day Balakireff asked permission of Peter to attach himself to the Guards of the Imperial Palace. The Czar consented, but added, —

"For any remissness of duty you will receive the same punishments as they."

"I will do my best," said Balakireff.

One night the Czar sent him wine from his table. He drank freely, and

THE COTTAGE OF PETER THE GREAT.

when the palace became still, fell asleep, as Peter supposed he would, at his post.

The punishment of a Guard for sleeping at his post was death.

Peter drew the jester's sword from its belt, and carried it away.

When Balakireff awoke, he was greatly terrified at finding his sword gone, for he knew his crime had been discovered.

He had a false sword, made of wood, and he hung this by his side and appeared at parade the next morning.

Peter appeared at the parade also. He presently began to storm about the untidy appearance of one of the men, and, apparently in a towering passion, exclaimed, —

"Captain Balakireff, draw your sword and cut that sloven down."

WILLIAM III., PRINCE OF ORANGE.

The poor jester put his hand on the hilt of the wooden sword.

He looked upward reverently, as though unwilling to do so dreadful a deed.

"Merciful Heaven!" he said. "Let my sword be turned to *wood*."

He drew the sword, and gazed at it as though a miracle had been wrought upon it.

The Czar fell into a fit of laughter, and Balakireff was allowed to escape punishment.

What a state of society do these anecdotes reveal, when any one's life was at the caprice of a brutal sovereign!

Peter's ambition was to advance Russia in mechanical arts, in the industries that produce wealth, and in military and naval greatness. He invited to his country skilled engineers, architects, and artillerymen from Austria, Venice, Prussia, and Holland. He himself visited the countries where the arts of civilization were making the most rapid progress. In disguise he travelled over Prussia and Holland; and at Amsterdam he worked for a time as a common shipwright. He afterwards visited William III. of England.

His curiosity was excessive. He wished to understand every art that he might transplant it in his own empire. One day, chancing to meet a lady on the street who had a fine watch, he called to her, —

"Stop, stop, and let me see it."

Peter had a son named Alexis, whom he expected to be his successor, and who had all of the bad and none of the heroic qualities of his father.

The wise man in the Hebrew Scriptures said that those who indulge in vice shall at last be holden by "the cords of their own sins." Indulgence in vice produces habits, and these habits become the governing power of life. The evil-doer becomes bound, self-imprisoned. His will power is lost.

We do not know of a more painful illustration of this truth than that furnished by Alexis. He inherited a love for sensual company and the intoxicating cup; and before he reached manhood he had so educated his evil passions that he came to care for nothing but further indulgence in vice. His excesses ruined his health, took away all resolution and ambition.

The Czar, seeing him tending to ruin, resolved to bring about a change in his character. He took him with him on his journeys to foreign capitals, and showed him the triumphs of art. But Alexis cared for none of these things; while his father was seeking to cultivate in him a feeling of national pride, he was only looking about him slyly for some occasion for a debauch.

The throne of all the Russias was less to him than the weakest opportunity to indulge his depraved passions.

His father chose a wife for him, — a lovely Polish princess, — thinking this would lead to reformation. But Alexis soon abandoned his beautiful wife for the company of an ignorant slave that he had purchased, named Afrosinia. The princess lived alone, in utter neglect, while Alexis was drinking and carousing with Afrosinia and his companions in vice. She died at last of a broken heart.

Peter was in despair.

He said to Alexis, —

"My reproofs have been fruitless. I have only lost my time and beaten the air. You do not so much as try to grow better. I will give you one trial more: if you do not improve your conduct, I will cut you off from the succession to the throne."

Alexis cared little for thrones or crowns. He answered, —

"If it is your majesty's pleasure to deprive me of the crown of Russia, your will be done. I even request it, as I do not think myself fit for the government. My memory is weakened. My mind and body are much decayed by the distempers to which I have been subject."

But although Alexis knew his vices were hurrying him to ruin, he did not seek to check their force. He resolved to follow them as long as he could, and then retire from the sight of the world to a convent.

There was a handsome peasant girl in Livonia by the name of Martha Rabe. She was left an orphan early, and was cared for by the parish clergyman.

There was a pie-boy in Moscow by the name of Alexander. In order to attract customers he used to sing songs. One day Peter heard him singing.

A MONASTERY IN NORTHERN RUSSIA.

He called him to him, and asked him how much he would take for the cakes, pies, and *basket*.

"I will sell you the cakes and pies, but the basket is not my own. I must return it to its owner. Still, your majesty can command me to give it up."

Peter was pleased with the answer, took the boy into his service, and at last made him Prince Menzikoff. Thus began a great and powerful Russian family.

Prince Menzikoff took Martha Rabe into his service. The Czar chanced to see her and was enamored of her. He at last married her, and she became Catherine I. of Russia. A son was born of this union; and Peter determined that this son, now that Alexis had proved himself utterly unworthy, should become his successor, unless Alexis would at once reform.

These facts of history read more like fiction than many wonder tales do. But we have now to give you the picture of the end of poor Alexis.

Peter wrote to him: —

"Either change your conduct, and labor to make yourself worthy of the succession, or else take the monastic vow."

Alexis answered: —

"I shall enter upon a monastic life."

On receiving this answer Peter resolved to visit him, and try once more to awaken his resolution and self-respect.

When Alexis heard he was coming, he took to his bed and pretended to be sick. He received his father in this way. Soon after the Czar had departed he was found carousing with his profligate associates.

The Czar went to Copenhagen. During his absence Alexis, taking with him his favorite slave, Afrosinia, fled to Vienna. Peter compelled the Austrian emperor to send him back; he gave him over to a council of state for trial; the council condemned him to death as a traitor, and the Czar was not unwilling the sentence should be executed.

The day of execution was at hand. Alexis trembled at the prospect of death. The past was a long career of shame; the future was dark, and the manner of the exchange of worlds to be terrible. His fears wrought upon him until he fell down in an apoplectic fit.

The Czar was sent for; he entered the room, and Alexis knew him. The latter began to weep.

"I have sinned against God and man," he said. "I hope I shall not live. I am unworthy to live."

He soon sank into the sleep of death. The Czar and Czarina attended the funeral; and a sermon was preached on the occasion from the text, "O Absalom, my son! my son Absalom!"

At the death-bed of Alexis even Peter was seen to weep. They were hopeless tears. Well would it have been if the father had set for his son a better example in his youth, for the faults of the son were those of the father, except that the one had a fiery ambition, and the other lacked all heroic feeling. It was a case of evil producing its own fruit.

Petersburg, the Russians call it, and sometimes Petropol.

Did you ever search for wild cranberries in a bog where the ground trembled under your feet, and you sprang from one tuft of grass or moss to another, lest you should sink in the spongy depths?

On just such a marsh as that, and in the latitude of southern Greenland, St. Petersburg is built. It occupies the shores and islands at the mouth of the Neva, that broad, swift river, which runs from Lake Ladoga, the largest lake in Europe, forty miles to the Gulf of Finland.

But why was such an unpromising site chosen for a great city?

At the beginning of the last century, when railways were unknown and good roads few and far between, Russia, with her immense territory, and her capital — Moscow — in its centre, was almost isolated, for at no point, except near the pole, did she touch the sea. To be sure there was the newly taken town of Azof, at the mouth of the Don; but hostile Tartars, under powerful khans, guarded the country between it and the Euxine, and below were the Turks, eager, as they are to-day, to thrust back the Muscovites if they dared to enter Moslem waters; so that, for all the good it did her, Azof might as well have been at the source as at the mouth of the river.

Her sovereign, Peter the Great, resolved to give her a port and navies and commerce, like those of the other nations of Europe; and having wrested from Sweden the region about the mouth of the Neva, in May, 1703, he began to build there his new capital.

What a labor it was! The shores and islands were swamps, hardly above the level of the water; but so determined was he that when the Finns pointed out to him a tree on whose trunk was marked the terrible height to which the waves sometimes rose when tide and river met, he cut it down with his own hands, and forbade their mentioning it again.

Whole forests were levelled for piles to drive into the mud, and endless ship-loads of stone brought for walls and embankments before the ground was solid enough to bear the weight of streets. Workmen were summoned thither from every part of the empire; but so malarious were these undrained morasses that it is said a hundred thousand men perished there in the building of the city.

Peter himself shared their hardships, living in a little cabin on one of the islands; and, although he had a natural dread of the sea, he would have no bridges made, because he wished to accustom his people to the use of boats.

In this high latitude the cold is of course severe. The brief summer goes like a dream. The Neva is frozen by the middle of October, and it is the last of April before it runs free again. For more than half the year there is snow,—snow everywhere; a bitter wind blows from off the steppes, sighing through the pines and the leafless birch-groves; and the whole aspect of nature is desolate and forlorn.

Indeed, St. Petersburg has a perpetual contest with the elements. It is always in danger of floods; and the long frosts crack its stones and unsettle the foundations of its houses, so that it is always undergoing repairs.

At first the Russians hated it, and only lived there because they were compelled to do so by the authority of Peter; but successive sovereigns have improved and embellished it, and now it is a great and splendid city, and the pride of the nation.

Let us stand in the mile-long *Ploschad*, the Admiralty Place on the south bank of the Neva (named from the vast building for naval purposes which bounds it on the north), and look about us.

That noble pile of reddish-brown Finland granite and bronze, surmounted by the huge gilded dome and shining cross, is the Cathedral of St. Isaac.

More than a million dollars were expended in driving piles into the ground to give it a firm foundation; and the richest mines of the Ourals have sent their precious stones and metals and marbles for the decoration of the interior, making it gorgeous with the vivid green of malachite, the deep blue of the lapis lazuli, the gleam of polished porphyry, and the glitter of gold and silver. Notice how the Russians, as they pass under its shadow, make with the thumb and the first two fingers of the right hand the sign of the cross upon their breasts.

ST. ISAAC'S CATHEDRAL.

If you should enter its lofty doors, which stand always open for the devout, you would see them prostrating themselves, and placing lighted tapers (small candles) by the shrines; for in their worship flame is the emblem of divinity and immortality, and in churches and private houses lamps are kept burning before the sacred pictures.

Just opposite St. Isaac's, and close to the river, look at the famous equestrian statue of Peter the Great. The boulder on which his horse is rearing, and which is larger than many a peasant's cottage, was

THE EXCHANGE.

brought with much trouble from a swamp several miles away, where it lay imbedded in the moss; and of the fragments which were cut or broken off in fitting it for the place, snuff-boxes, cane-heads, and other small articles were made, and sold at fabulous prices, the people thinking there was a miracle in the finding of the stone.

Away at the other end of the Place rises the Alexander Column of

Finland granite, adorned with bronze, erected by the Emperor Nicholas to the memory of his brother, Alexander I. How it towers upon its pedestal, the angel on its summit lifting the cross at a height of more than one hundred and fifty feet above its base! And what do you think furnished the metal of which the bronze was made? Captured Turkish cannon.

The shaft alone, the largest stone which has been reared in modern days, has a weight of four hundred tons; and in order to support the whole, six successive rows of piles were driven into the ground on which it stands.

Beyond the Column, that stately pile, built also by Nicholas, is the Winter Palace, and the residence of the Czar. The old palace, which stood upon the same spot, and was burned in 1837, must have been a strange, irregular structure; for I have heard that in a remote corner of it a soldier of the guard had his quarters, and kept his cow upon the roof.

The present palace contains some of the most splendid rooms in the world, finished with gold and malachite, and rich in every beautiful thing which the art of man has devised. During its occupancy by the Court, several thousand people inhabit it, and the most sumptuous entertainments are often given.

You would think yourself at the equator, rather than so near the pole, if you could look in on one of these brilliant evenings when royalty, nobility, and official rank — the Romanoffs, the Stroganoffs, the Galitzins, and representatives of many another famous name — are assembled here, sitting at supper under the shade of orange-trees and tall ferns, that make the banquet-hall a bower of green.

Whichever way you look in this Admiralty Place, you see noble buildings for purposes of state, imposing monuments, and palaces belonging to the royal family and the nobles.

From it the wide streets radiate like a fan, the handsomest being the *Nevski Prospekt* (Neva Prospective), the fashionable drive and

NEVSKI PROSPEKT.

promenade. In this street is the Kazan Church, built by Alexander I., at a cost of three millions of dollars, and to which the royal family repair for special religious services, such as thanksgiving for the Czar's escape from assassination in April, 1866, and for the safe arrival of the Princess Dagmar of Denmark, to wed the heir, the Grand-Duke Alexander, in September of the same year.

That enormous building a little further down is the Great Bazaar, in whose shops, with those of the adjacent markets, all the wares of

NICHOLAS BRIDGE.

Russia and of Europe are for sale; and at its eastern extremity, past the bend where stands the station of the Moscow railway, those graceful domes and towers rise from the Monastery of Alexander Nevski, one of Russia's holiest shrines.

Look a little to the north and see those five azure domes studded with golden stars, and lying like flowers against the sky. They mark the Smolnoi Church and school for girls, founded by the Empress Maria, grandmother of the present emperor.

Observe how many of the houses have their roofs painted bright green. These, with the blue and gold of the cupolas beneath their shining crosses, and the little gardens of bloom — scarlet geraniums, fuchsias, pinks, roses — in the wide, south-looking windows, give the charm of color under the dull and often hazy sky. For our full sunshine never lights these northern heavens, and there is a certain dimness even in the clearest day.

Four bridges cross the Neva from this larger city of the mainland to that of the islands. Three of them are built of boats; the fourth, the Nicholas Bridge, is a superb, solid structure of granite and iron.

On the small island nearly opposite the Winter Palace, that massive pile, with its slender gilded spire almost four hundred feet in air, is the Fortress and Cathedral of St. Peter and St. Paul; and at every event of importance to the city, such as the first entrance of the Princess Dagmar, or an alarming rise of the water, its cannon boom over the Neva.

In this cathedral sleep Peter the Great and his successors, under tombs of white marble, surmounted by a golden cross, while the dungeons of the fortress are used for prisoners of state.

What horror to be shut in these gloomy cells, with their memories of grief and crime, and to hear the waves surge and dash against the walls, — the waves which twice within a century have almost undermined the foundations!

THE ASSASSINATION OF THE CZAR.

CHAPTER XVI.

THE ASSASSINATION OF THE CZAR.

THE ASSASSINATION OF THE CZAR. — FUNERAL OF THE CZAR. — INAUGURATION OF ALEXANDER III. — THE CLASS BIDS FAREWELL TO RUSSIA.

REAT changes have taken place in Russia since the time we have assigned to the journey in the Orient.

Alexander II. was then on the throne; a czar that history will love to remember as the emancipator of the Greek Christians in Turkey, and of the serfs of his own broad dominions.

But the people of Russia wish to be emancipated from the absolute power of the Czar. They desire the protection that a constitution affords. The Nihilists in this respect represent the Russian people, though in respect to religious and social affairs they do not express the popular sentiment.

All political efforts to secure a constitutional government have been repressed. The leaders of republican sentiment have been arrested and sent to Siberia. This repression has strengthened the Nihilists, and has led them to the belief that there is no hope of freedom for Russia but by the destruction of the czars.

From this state of affairs has come a terrible tragedy whose story we must here tell.

A party of young conspirators was organized several years ago for the purpose of killing the Czar. One of their secret places of meeting was a cheese shop, from which a mine was dug, which was intended for the destruction of the Imperial Palace.

The police visited this shop while the mine was preparing.

"What have you here?" asked an official of a conspirator, pointing to a barrel.

"Only cheese," was the reply.

"And here?"

"Cheese."

The police went away.

Both barrels contained dynamite.

Among these conspirators was Sophie Picoffsky (Sophie Loofa Peroffskaya), the daughter of a former governor of St. Petersburg, and niece to an officer in the Imperial Court. She joined the Revolutionists in 1872. She was exiled in 1878, but escaped.

The conspirators determined to assassinate the Czar by the use of explosive materials. They attempted to blow up a train on which he was travelling, and afterwards the Imperial Palace.

One of their plans was to throw under his carriage, when he was riding, explosive bombs.

It was expected that the Emperor would be on the street in his carriage on the 13th of March.

The conspirators resolved that this day should end his life.

Two bombs were carefully made, and intrusted to Sophie Picoffsky. She brought them to a place where the conspirators had agreed to meet, concealing them in a bundle.

She said, —

"If the Emperor passes down the Sadovaya, explode the mine. On the explosion of the mine, run to the spot, and insure the death of the Emperor if he be not already killed.

"If the Imperial carriage go by the way of the Catherine Canal, wait the victim there. I will give the sign for the throwing of the bombs."

THE CZAR LYING IN STATE

The Imperial carriage passed by the way of the canal.

It was a gray March day. Sophie Picoffsky stood in the sharp air waiting the approach of her victim. The Imperial carriage came sweeping towards the canal.

She gave the signal to the conspirators. One bomb was thrown. There was a fearful explosion. But the Emperor was not killed.

The Emperor attempted to leave the carriage.

Sophie Picoffsky gave another signal.

A second bomb was thrown; and the body of Alexander II. lay a shattered mass on the frozen earth.

The conspirators were all young. Sophie Picoffsky was but twenty-seven. They were executed. Each met death calmly. They regarded themselves as martyrs to the cause of liberty.

The funeral of the Czar was one of the most magnificent and pathetic pageants that Russia ever saw. St. Petersburg was hung with black. Salvos of artillery signalled the forming and the moving of the procession. The white standard of the murdered monarch was unfurled over the fortress, and all the bells of the city tolled.

Mr. Sala, the English correspondent, after describing the forming and the advance of the immense procession, gives a graphic picture of the most impressive incidents of the scene: —

"Following the priests came the gorgeous catafalque, on which rested the coffin, under a rich canopy of gold, surmounted by white ostrich plumes.

"We were asking 'What next, — and next?' when the hearse came suddenly in view; and the prodigious mass of humanity rapidly, as a flash of lightning, so to speak, uncovered.

"It was a most wondrous sight to behold, — that black sea of hats and caps transformed into an immense expanse of pale, upturned faces.

"The funeral car was a bier of ebony and silver, on wheels with heavily carved silver spokes, and a superstructure of black and silver.

The whole was canopied by superb material encircling the columns of the bier. The coffin of the illustrious deceased was almost hidden by a golden pall, lined with white satin; and the vast car itself was drawn by eight black horses, completely shrouded in sable draperies.

"Four general *aides-ac-camp* stood one at each corner of the catafalque, the polished metal wheels of which glistened in the sunlight. Sixteen general officers held the silken cords of the canopy. Behind the bier of his murdered sire walked Alexander III., in his imperial solitude, bearing alone his filial sorrow and his state cares."

Alexander, the eldest living son of the Czar, succeeds Alexander II. on the Imperial throne of Russia, and assumes the title of Alexander III.

He is, next to the kings of Bavaria and Spain, the youngest sovereign in Europe, being just thirty-six. His elder brother, Nicholas, a young man of great promise, died some fifteen years ago of consumption. Nicholas was betrothed to the lovely young Princess Dagmar of Denmark; and some time after his death the same young lady became the wife of his brother Alexander, and is now Empress of Russia.

Alexander III., both in personal appearance and in his traits of character, is a very different man from his father. He is not, like the late Czar, a strikingly handsome person. His features are large and irregular; his figure is rather solid and muscular than, like that of his father, graceful and elegant. He has a proud, haughty, fierce look; and in his high and stern bearing more resembles the stalwart and despotic Nicholas, his grandfather.

More like Nicholas, too, than the second Alexander in his tastes, he is a true soldier,— fond of parade and of war; adventurous, courageous, and truculent. He has not inherited his father's timid and retiring spirit. He is fearless and bold; and bids fair to rule with a strong hand, relying rather upon himself than upon the counsels of others.

Alexander III., indeed, has seen some rough service in the field.

INAUGURATION OF ALEXANDER III.

He held a command in the army in the Turkish war; and on more than one field displayed great impetuosity and valor. Like a true warrior of the hardy North, he freely shared the privations and hardships of his troops; the marks of this are seen in his frost-bitten left hand, and a large scar which somewhat disfigures his weather-beaten face.

It is pleasant to add that the new Czar's private character is stainless, and that his tastes are domestic. He is devoted to his lovely Danish wife, and to his fine, healthy children. This is one of the few traits in which he resembles the late Czar.

The late Czar was a devoted friend of his uncle, the German Emperor, and was ardently attached to the German people, among whom he was educated. This fact had an important bearing on the course of European courts, and cemented the alliance between the two great empires. This alliance enabled Germany to conquer France, and Russia to subdue Turkey, by holding other powers in check.

Alexander III., however, is supposed to be far from friendly towards Germany. He is said to better like France and the French. If this turns out to be true, it may have a startling influence on the relations of European powers. A new war between France and Germany — which is always more or less probable — might find Russia on the side of the young Republic instead of on that of the German Empire.

The Class left St. Petersburg for England, visiting Cronstadt, the naval station of Russia and one of the summer resorts of the Russians, on the way. Master Lewis had expected to meet Mr. Beal and the party of young tourists from Germany in London, but he found that they had gone to Queenstown by the way of Ireland, and would take the steamer from that port.

Farewell, Russia! The grandest destiny of the empires of the East is before thee. Thy struggle for Liberty is but begun. The storm of Revolution is yet to come. In other nations of Europe the battles for freedom have been fought and won. Thy battle-fields are before thee. A constitution is to be gained; an elective assembly, each member of which shall be a ruler, is to be established. Scenes like those of the French Revolution may darken the future; but thou art to be free from the Neva to the Volga. Thou wilt yet cover the

CRONSTADT.

Caspian and the Euxine with thy fleets; thou wilt yet march forth from the Caucasus to control the destinies of Asia; the city of Constantine will yet be the head of thy ancient Church, and over St. Sophia the cross shall blaze where the crescent shines. The histories of other nations of the East are drawing to a close; thine is but just begun.

www.ingramcontent.com/pod-product-compliance
Lightning Source LLC
Chambersburg PA
CBHW022046230426
43672CB00008B/1082